09-AIE-715   APR 4 '07

TRAVELING WITH CHE GUEVARA

"Yesterday we crossed the imaginary but real line that separates Argentina from Chile. I can't say that, in the words of the pasodoble, 'I turned back, my eyes full of tears,' because although I was leaving my motherland and loved ones behind, there were others to love and new countries to see as our compass pointed north to the rest of Latin America.

"If anything saddened us, it was that we clearly witnessed, yet again, as in so many other parts of our beloved Argentina, the need for radical sociopolitical change that would end man's exploitation of man and the exploitation of our country by international cartels."

—From Alberto Granado's journal,
February 14, 1952

"This is documentary writing with an unmistakable political bite, but it also contains comic and mythical elements: the three major characters—Che Guevara, Dr. Granado and the clapped-out motorcycle—have much in common with Cervantes' fictional Don Quixote, Sancho Panza, and Rocinante....What is surprising in these fiery young ideologues is their passionate interest in poetry, music and the visual arts....It is their restless curiosity about the world in general—and not simply the world of politics—that makes this journal worth reading in detail....The excitements and fascinations of this book are many."

—Book review by Andrew Biswell,
Scotland on Sunday, 2003

HIGH SCHOOL
SEATTLE, WA

Alberto Granado was born in Hernando in the province of Córdoba, Argentina, on 8 August 1922. In 1943 he was jailed for his participation in a political movement against the dictatorship of General Juan Perón. He earned a master's degree in chemistry at the University of Córdoba in 1946 and in Biochemistry in 1948. Between 29 December 1951 and 26 July 1952 he traveled all over South America with Ernesto Guevara.

When the Venezuelan dictator Pérez Jiménez was ousted in 1958 he was put in charge of the reorganization of the School of Bio-analysis at the University of Caracas where he worked until 1961. He went to live in Cuba in March 1961 where he became professor of medical biochemistry in the Faculty of Medicine at the University of Havana.

In 1962 he was a member of the group of professors who founded Cuba's Second Faculty of Medicine at the University of Santiago. In 1967 he was transferred to Havana where he took part in the creation of the Agricultural and Stockbreeding Department at the National Centre for Scientific Research. He was one of the founders of the National Health Centre for Stockbreeding and Farming where he was Director of the Department of Genetics until 1994 when he retired. In 2002 Alberto Granado served as an adviser to director Walter Salles throughout the filming of *The Motorcycle Diaries*.

Lucía Álvarez de Toledo grew up and was educated in Argentina, and was awarded a scholarship at the University of Delhi. Having worked as a journalist and broadcaster she settled in London in 1968 and established herself as a professional interpreter and translator, working at the highest levels for governments, corporations and international institutions. Her background, knowledge of South America and long-standing friendship with Alberto Granado have enabled her to bring a unique understanding to the first English-language translation of this book.

TRAVELING WITH CHE GUEVARA

The Making of a Revolutionary

ALBERTO GRANADO

Translated by Lucía Álvarez de Toledo

Newmarket Press • New York

For Che
Alberto Granado and Lucía Álvarez de Toledo would like
to thank Margaret Hanbury and Anne McLean for their
support and commitment.

Copyright © 1978, 2004 by Alberto Granado
Translation and chronology copyright © Lucía Álvarez de Toledo 2003,
2004
Photographs courtesy of Lucía Álvarez de Toledo

All rights reserved. This book may not be reproduced, in whole or in part,
in any form, without written permission. Inquiries should be addressed to
Permissions Department, Newmarket Press, 18 East 48th Street, New York,
NY 10017.

First published in the United States of America by Newmarket Press

First Edition

10   9   8   7   6   5   4   3   2   1
ISBN 1-55704-639-5 (paperback)

10   9   8   7   6   5   4   3   2   1
ISBN 1-55704-640-9 (hardcover)

Library of Congress Cataloging-in-Publication Data

Granado, Alberto, 1922-
   [Con el Che por Sudamirica. English]
   Traveling with Che Guevara : the making of a revolutionary / Alberto Granado ;
translated by Lucía Álvarez de Toledo. —1st ed.
       p. cm.
   ISBN 1-55704-640-9 (hardcover : alk. paper) — ISBN 1-55704-639-5 (pbk. : alk.
paper)
   1. Guevara, Ernesto, 1928-1967—Friends and associates. 2. Granado, Alberto,
1922—Diaries. 3. Scientists—South America—Diaries. 4. South America—
Description and travel. 5. South America—Social conditions. I. Title.

F2224.G6813 2004
   918.04'35—dc22

                                                        2004018373

QUANTITY PURCHASES
Companies, professional groups, clubs, and other organizations may qualify
for special terms when ordering quantities of this title. For information,
write Special Sales Department, Newmarket Press, 18 East 48th Street, New
York, NY 10017; call (212) 832-3575; fax (212) 832-3629; or e-mail
mailbox@newmarketpress.com.

www.newmarketpress.com

Manufactured in the United States of America.

Contents

Translator's note   vii
Preface (2004) to the American Edition:
    The Return of the Sedentary Gypsy   ix
Preface (2003) to the British edition   xiii
Foreword   xvii
Map   xxi
Itinerary: principal stops   xxii

Prologue   I
An almost ill-fated departure   3
The pampa of the Ranqueles   11
The perfect exploitation machine   26
In Araucania   32
More calamities: volunteer firemen   39
Farewell to "Poderosa II"—from bikers to stowaways   48
One side of the coin—the Yankee copper mines   56
In the land where Lafertté fought   67
In the land of the Incas   74
Machu Picchu at last   85
To the Huambo leprosarium   96

Photo section follows page 104

To the Peruvian rain forest 111
Ernesto cannot tell a lie 121
The Amazon and its people 128
En route to the San Pablo leprosarium 140
Science in the jungle 143
An unusual birthday 151
An unforgettable send-off 160
From leprologists to soccer players 169
Bogotá—a city under siege 175
In the land of Bolívar 191
A family gathering 197

Epilogue 201
Chronology 205

Translator's note

In 1952 Ernesto Guevara and his friend Alberto Granado, the owner of the famous motorcycle, set off to travel around South America. Guevara, who was twenty-three, was about to graduate as a doctor. Granado, six years his senior, was already a doctor and a biochemist. The trip was Alberto's idea but Ernesto had never needed much persuasion to embark on an adventure.

Both men kept diaries of the journey. Guevara's was published by his estate long after his death in Bolivia in 1967 while Granado's was first published in Spanish in Cuba in 1978. In Spanish, Italian and French both diaries were published together. Granado had the advantage over Guevara of being still alive and therefore was able to revise his version of events and produce a more complete picture. Also, at twenty-nine he already had a political conscience. But what really makes Granado's account of the journey so riveting is that as well as describing the journey, he is reporting his friend's reaction to their adventures, thus unwittingly giving us a candid picture of the man who was to become Che Guevara—Latin America's foremost revolutionary hero who later would say of himself: "I was born in Argentina, I fought in Cuba, and I became a revolutionary in Guatemala." He was to die in Bolivia, fighting for the oppressed of the continent, having said that he had never felt like a foreigner in any country of Latin America. The journey described in this book marks the beginning of that discovery—that he was one with the poor and downtrodden of the Americas.

Later he would explain in his writings that because of the precarious conditions in which he traveled he was able to stay in touch with the people and see at close quarters the poverty, hunger and disease that afflicted them. It was during this journey that he realized that as a future doctor he would not be able to help these people because of the political make-up of the continent. It would not be enough to cure the effects, it was the causes that had to be attacked. So the man who had been an admirer of Gandhi for his belief in non-violence was to turn to arms to pursue his objective of liberating the poor and the disenfranchised of the Americas.

And yet, Guevara was a man full of humor and mirth, capable of huge pranks and practical jokes. He loved parties and drinking and women. The Guevara de la Sernas were a formidable clan who stayed close and united even after Ernesto became a Cuban public figure. And Alberto Granado, who at the end of this journey, had settled and married in Venezuela, was to join him in Cuba to support the revolution, not as a soldier, but as a scientist.

Walter Salles's film *The Motorcycle Diaries*—starring Gael García Bernal, Mia Maestro and Rodrigo de la Serna—is based on the two diaries, and Alberto Granado was on location at Salles's side throughout the shoot as an adviser thus bringing to the cinematic narration of the story the true flavor of the Latin America of the fifties.

L. Á. de T.
February 2003

Preface (2004) to the American Edition

The Return of the Sedentary Gypsy

My friend Ernesto Guevara de la Serna nicknamed me The Sedentary Gypsy because I was always dreaming up lengthy journeys for us to make while at the same time wishing to stay at home with my family and friends. He knew me well.

Today, almost sixty years later and owing to a whole range of different circumstances The Sedentary Gypsy has returned to the scene, leaving behind the peace and quiet of his home in the agreeable city of La Habana, where he has spent the past forty-three years surrounded by the warmth of his friends, students and colleagues and the love of his children and grandchildren.

How can I explain such a radical change in my life? I believe there is only one answer: I retired from my scientific career in order to give way to the new generation who are now mature enough to make their own contribution in the field of genetics. And I imagined a period of quiet. But one must be true to oneself—and the ever-present desire to see new skies even when it really meant revisiting skies that I had seen before....

How did the marvelous adventure that I describe begin?

Let me give you a brief summary of what happened: when in 1978, after the avalanche of propaganda caused by the death of my friend Ernesto Che Guevara had abated and false friends and pseudo-historians had finally calmed down, I decided to publish my diary of the journey that Ernesto and I had embarked on together.

The purpose of publishing it was to show the world that Ernesto was a man of flesh and blood and not a sort of mythological being, as some unscrupulous friends would have him appear, and above all, the enemies of my friend's revolutionary ideas, who by transforming him into a myth hoped to prove that it was impossible to follow his example.

Following the success in 1992 of the Italian edition of both our diaries in a single volume called *Latinoamericana*, the long standing dream of transferring to the screen our wonderful journey across our long-suffering and beloved South America finally became a reality.

The opportunity then arose for me to act as a consultant during the shooting of the film and the documentary made about the film that was shot on location simultaneously. I had a choice between battling against my eighty years and going back on the road to relive the trip or staying and keeping company with other old people and doing the research for my new literary project on the similarities between Martí and Guevara.

But my indecision did not last long because I felt compelled to be with the actors and the director on location to ensure that fiction came as close as possible to the events that had taken place half a century earlier.

At the same time life allowed me to fulfill one of my most cherished dreams: to take my family to the places that I had so often told them about.

As has so often been the case, real life surpassed my expectations, and the reception I got from the actors, the director and the crew was fabulous and almost all my advice and suggestions were readily accepted. Of course that happened after an exchange of ideas and opinions which made me learn two things: the first is that once more fortune had brought together men and women of great sensitivity to make a film which is faithful to the spirit of what both Ernesto and I had poured into our diaries. And the second thing is how difficult and time-consuming it is to make a good job of shooting even apparently very simple scenes—for example, the scene in which Ernesto and I bid farewell to our beloved Poderosa II, a scene which in real life only took a few brief minutes, required more than half an hour before the director was satisfied. The most extraordinary thing is that gradually I realized that each time a scene was repeated it drew closer and closer to reality.

I also learned that although every crewmember seemed to be only interested in their own task, these individual efforts collectively resulted in creation of great quality.

As my readers will imagine, being the spectator of such a journey half a century later enabled me to relive moments of emotion with my loved ones who were accompanying me. But nothing was as deeply felt as the meeting with several of the patients afflicted with leprosy who remembered our stay at the leprosarium of San Pablo—and this peaked when the youngest of them (who back in 1952 was fifteen years old) recalled the moment in which I shook his hand without putting on gloves when we met and said affectionately: "After you two visited our hospital, people were kinder to us."

What greater reward could one ask from life?

Alberto Granado, Mial[1]
La Habana, March 2004

---

[1] Mial: a nickname given to the author by Guevara. It is a contraction of Mi Alberto, which is what his grandmother used to call him.

Preface (2003) to the British edition

When a quarter of a century ago—in 1978—I wrote the foreword to the first edition of my book *Con el Che por Sudamérica*, I was only interested in bringing to the attention of the public both the greatness and the misery of Latin America as seen through the eyes of a dreamer, albeit one who was also a realist.

More than ten years had lapsed since the assassination of my beloved traveling companion, and the propagandist pyrotechnics created around his person by the self-appointed friends and the usual opportunists had died down. I thought it was high time to make known a very important facet of the life of the man who had already become the New Man for millions of women and men, the majority of them young, who saw in his example the path to follow if they were to create a fairer world.

My purpose at the time was to show, through my retelling of the story, that El Pelao (Baldy) Guevara of the motorcycle trip, Che Guevara of the Sierra Maestra and the great revolutionary leader, was just a man who was true to his principles.

But once again life has gone beyond my wildest dreams and here I am, fifty years after that trip, when luck, fate or whatever you want to call it affords me the opportunity of seeing a youthful reincarnation of myself at twenty-nine—in the person of the Argentine actor Rodrigo de la Serna, who relives episodes that took place in the last

century and that are being re-created by Walter Salles for
the film *The Motorcycle Diaries.*

Of all the episodes that I have lived through again there
are four in the film that, for different reasons, have moved
me more than I can say.

The first one in southern Chile was when I saw the re-
enacting of the scene in which Ernesto, who had had too
much to drink and was reacting to the provocative behavior of the wife of the mechanic who had tried to fix our
motorcycle, attempted to leave the dance hall with her;
but the woman, who was willing at the beginning, realizing that she was being watched, changed her mind and
resisted his advances. Of course, he was in such a state
that he was unable to change tack and that resulted in a
tug-of-war between the two, which attracted the attention of the husband and his friends. Ernesto and I were
forced to leave at high speed in order to avoid an unpleasant incident.

The other episode in Chile was the scene in which I bid
farewell to the motorcycle, wrapped up in a tent as if it
were a shroud, and thus leave my companion of so many
adventures, abandoning it there.

Meeting up again with Zoraida Boluarte was really
moving as she had been our guardian angel for the dura-
tion of our trip. She had been able to find us lodgings and
food, due to her position as a social assistant at the Guía
leprosarium, and had made us a present of a portable cook-
er, which was extremely useful during the Amazonian
section of the voyage.

It is not easy to describe the mixture of joy and nostal-
gia that I felt on finding myself again in Lima, a city that
taught both Ernesto and me so much, through the person
of Dr. Hugo Pesce. He was the man who not only briefed
us on the latest developments in the fields of allergies and
asthma, but also introduced us to the most authentic of

Peruvian poets, César Vallejo,[1] as well as to José Mariátegui,[2] a true Marxist of Latin American origins, with whose
philosophy both Ernesto and I fully identified.

But the zenith of all emotions—almost impossible to
describe—was my arrival at Santa María, a village near the
town of Iquitos, where a section of the San Pablo leprosarium was rebuilt in order to film one of the most crucial
stages of our now historic journey. There I met up with a
group of patients who at the time of our trip were between
fourteen and twenty years of age and who remembered in
great detail our stay at the leprosarium, as well as the fact
that we revolutionized the life of the inhabitants of the
hospital and of the patients, who could not believe that
two healthy men were prepared to share hugs, games and
food with those afflicted by the fearful Hansen bacillus;
and how the workers and doctors were astonished by this
new way of facing the need to improve health by means of
human affection without prejudice or fear.

But the most important fact, and the real reason that
prompted me to include this preface, is that in each of the
countries where the film was shot, it was done using local
bit players, workers and advisers for each category, thus
creating jobs at a time when there is massive unemploy-
ment as a result of the neo-liberal policies of those countries' governments.

And a further cause for satisfaction is the fact that all
the installations built at Santa María—the electricity supply, the meeting rooms, the pathways made of timber, the
distribution of running water, all the grid that provides
lighting to the village and all that was built for the film—

[1] César Vallejo (1892–1938), Peruvian poet, journalist, Communist militant
born in Santiago de Chuco, whose *Los Heraldos Negros* marked the dawn of a
new poetry in Peru.
[2] José Carlos Mariátegui (1894–1930), Peruvian Marxist thinker who was among
the first to blend nationalist and indigenous thought with international
Marxism.

remain in place for the enjoyment of the local inhabitants, and as a result will enhance the living conditions of each and every one of them.

So it can be said that history once again proves that one should be true to one's principles and beliefs.

Ever on to victory.

Alberto Granado, Mial
Havana, February 2003

Foreword

It's hard to pinpoint exactly when we came up with the idea for the trip. Literature played an important part. The urge to travel grew from reading Ciro Alegría's[4] books *The Golden Serpent*, *The Hungry Dogs* and *Broad and Alien Is the World*, all of which I had eagerly devoured.

I needed to see the world, but first I wanted to see Latin America, my own long-suffering continent—not through the eyes of a tourist, interested only in landscapes, comforts and fleeting pleasures, but with the eyes and spirit of one of the people, someone wanting to know about the continent's beauty, its riches, the men and women who live there, as well as Latin America's enemies, within and without, who exploit and impoverish us.

So from 1940 on, "the trip" became a journey through South America. Two years later, in 1942, Ernesto Guevara de la Serna—El Pelao, or Baldy, of my youth—came onto the scene, joining my usual audience of parents and brothers. With his natural irony and genius for criticism and argument, Pelao added a fresh note to our routine discussions of the Utopian journey.

Though barely fourteen years old, Pelao's uncommon acumen (a perspicacity he retained throughout his extraordinary life) allowed him to see that while for my parents and even my brothers the journey was little more than an agreeable topic of conversation, a pretext for widening our

[4] Ciro Alegría (1909–67), Peruvian writer and journalist. In *Broad and Alien Is the World* (1941) he depicts the suffering and exploitation of the Peruvian Indians.

knowledge of geography and politics, for me it was as real and tangible as the fact that I would one day become a biochemist, an honest scientist who would not sell out.

From that year on, Ernesto backed all my ideas and projects. Almost a decade passed before the plan became a reality, and whenever he detected a weakening in my resolve he would chime in with his refrain, "So, what about the trip, then?" I had only one answer, "Anything can go wrong, except that."

My friendship with Ernesto grew year by year, and our need to embark on the journey became more imperative.

The main events of that decade pass through my mind as if glimpsed through a kaleidoscope: the student struggles in defense of democratic, bourgeois freedom, threatened at the time by our own local Nazism, which—dressed up as nationalism—seemed to be taking over the country; the persecution and imprisonment of the real champions of the Argentine people; the clash between students and reactionary teachers, which spurred us to do better than those who kowtowed to gain favoritism.

It was during those years that Ernesto and I had become aware of the Soviet Union and its titanic struggle against the Nazi hordes trying to wipe the world's first socialist country off the face of the earth. In our eyes, Stalingrad, Leningrad, Brest and Moscow took on a new dimension. The heroism of the Soviet people could not be silenced by the alleged defenders of freedom and democracy.

The war years revealed the dishonesty of the capitalist press as their tissue of lies about the "red terror" and popular unrest vanished in the face of the unity of the people, the government and the Soviet Communist Party.

In 1945, I got my first appointment as a junior practitioner. This gave me my first opportunity to work in research, something I've never given up, although from time to time life has imposed other duties. A year later, I began to work in the J. J. Puente Leprosarium, in Córdoba. A fascinating world opened up before me.

The scourge of leprosy forces its victims out of society and at the same time makes them particularly sensitive and grateful. Anyone who has seen a leprosarium cannot but be won over by such a community of outcasts. During this period, Ernesto and I stayed in touch. By now his nickname El Pelao was replaced by Fúser—short for Furibundo, or Furious Guevara Serna—a tribute to his tenacity and fearlessness at rugby, the sport that, like soccer before it and shooting afterward, now filled our few free hours.

One day Fúser arrived in the remote hospital where I worked, hundreds of miles from Buenos Aires, on a bike with a motor fit only for the paved avenues of the city, but which Ernesto, with his determination and courage, had brought across plains, mountains and deserts.

Around this time I bought my "Poderosa II," a powerful Norton 500 cc motorcycle, named after "Poderosa I," the bike I'd used day in and day out during my student years for distributing leaflets at demonstrations and then eluding my police pursuers, as well as for outings to the rivers, lakes and mountains of my native Córdoba.

My sporadic meetings with Pelao confirmed how much we had in common. Literature gave us a lot to talk about. Around this time, a group of North American authors were first published in Argentina, among them Erskine Caldwell, Sinclair Lewis and William Faulkner, who laid bare the hypocrisy of American capitalist society and its discrimination against Hispanics and blacks.

Our interpretations of the works of Sartre and Camus, with their philosophical and political implications, gave rise to further discussion as we camped under starry skies, sharing maté, ideas and dreams around a cozy camp fire. Almost ten years went by in this way, seeing each other now and again; but rather than deter us, the passage of time gave us more and more reasons for undertaking our long-desired journey through Latin America.

Alberto Granado, Mial
Havana, October 1978

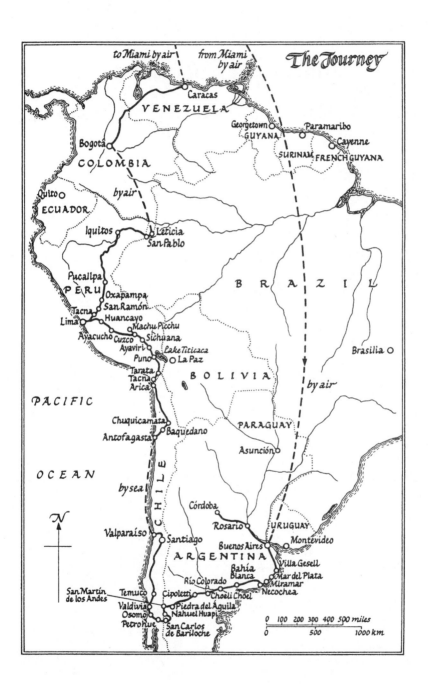

The Journey

to Miami by air — from Miami by air

VENEZUELA
Caracas

Georgetown GUYANA Paramaribo
Bogotá SURINAM Cayenne
COLOMBIA FRENCH GUYANA

Quito
ECUADOR
by air

Iquitos Leticia
San Pablo

Pucallpa
PERU
Oxapampa
Tacna San Ramón
Lima Huancayo
Machu Picchu
Ayacucho Cuzco Sicuana
Ayaviri
Puno Lake Titicaca
Tarata La Paz
Tacna
Arica BOLIVIA

BRAZIL

Brasilia

PACIFIC

Chuquicamata
Antofagasta Baquedano
PARAGUAY

by air

OCEAN

Asunción

by sea

Córdoba
Rosario URUGUAY
Valparaíso Santiago Montevideo
Buenos Aires
ARGENTINA
Villa Gesell
Bahía Mar del Plata
Blanca
Río Colorado Miramar
San Martín Temuco Cipoletti Necochea
de los Andes Choeli Choel
Valdivia Piedra del Águila
Osorno Nahuel Huapi
Petrohue San Carlos
de Bariloche

0 100 200 300 400 500 miles
0 500 1000 km

Itinerary: principal stops

ARGENTINA

Córdoba, 29 December 1951
Villa Gesell, 6 January
Miramar, 13 January
Necochea, 14 January
Bahía Blanca, 16–21 January
Choele Choel, 25 January
Piedra del Aguila, 29 January
San Martín de los Andes, 31 January
Lake Nahuel Huapí, 8 February
Bariloche, 11 February

CHILE

Peulla, 14 February
Lautaro, 21 February
Los Ángeles, 27 February
Santiago de Chile, 1 March
Valparaíso, 7 March
On board the *San Antonio*, 8–10 March
Antofagasta, 11 March
Baquedano, 12 March
Chuquicamata, 13–15 March
Iquique, 20 March
Arica, 22 March

PERU

Tacna, 24 March
Sicuani, 30 March
Cuzco, 31 March
Machu Picchu, 5 April
Cuzco, 6–7 April
Abancay, 11 April
Huancarama, 13 April
Huambo, 14 April
Huancarama, 15 April
Andahuaylas, 16–19 April
Ayacucho, 22 April
La Merced, 25–26 April
Oxapampa to San Ramón, 27 April
San Ramón, 28 April
Tarma, 30 April
Lima, 1–19 May
El Rancho, 19 May
On board *La Cenepa*, 25 May
The Amazon River, 26–31 May
Iquitos, 1–5 June
On board *El Cisne*, 6–7 June
The leprosarium of San Pablo, 8–20 June
On board *Mambo-Tango* on the Amazon River, 20–22 June

COLOMBIA

Leticia, 23 June–1 July, leaving by plane and stopping at
Tres Esquinas in transit
Bogotá, 2–10 July
Cúcuta, 12–13 July

VENEZUELA

San Cristóbal, 14 July
Between Barquisimeto and Corona, 16 July
Caracas, 17–26 July

Prologue

Caracas, 26 July 1952

Their hands, clasped in farewell, refuse to let go. They both try with little success to hide their emotions. Many of the two young men's dreams have been fulfilled and many more have yet to happen, which makes this goodbye difficult. Together they have cleared paths, surmounting obstacles that stood obstinately in their way. One of these obstacles has just been successfully overcome.

In the end, almost at the same time, the hands part, giving way to a swift embrace. Then a brief farewell to hide the emotion they both feel.

"I'll be waiting for you, Fúser."

"We'll get together again, Mial."

Mial sits on the wall between the runway and loading area, full of horses on their way to Miami. He watches Fúser grow smaller and smaller as he makes his way toward the huge cargo plane. It had been impossible to tell just how huge it was until now, measured against the tiny figure of his friend, who starts to climb up the ramp where the racehorses had been hoisted minutes before. Halfway, he turns his head and waves his right hand in farewell.

In response, Mial leaps to his feet, all his feigned indifference disappearing in an instant. He waves his arms and, defying the distance that muffles his voice, shouts, "Bye,

Fúser. I'll be waiting for you, Pelao. Study hard, Ernesto. Chau, chau."

The noise of the closing hatches is immediately followed by the roar of the engines. A minute or two later the plane passes over Mial's head. In a movement by now second nature to him, he drops down onto the lawn beside the wall of Maiquetía airport. He takes a notebook carefully covered in red paper out of a battered knapsack, rests his back against the wall and begins to read.

An almost ill-fated departure

Córdoba, 29 December 1951

Everything began and proceeded quickly and efficiently, which is how I usually do things. Time has erased the date, but the scene is as vivid and fresh as ever.

It's a sunlit October afternoon. The first spring tendrils and leaves on the vine climbing my family home tried to shade my faithful companion of trips across the pampas and mountains—my old motorbike, "Poderosa II." My brother Tomás was sitting on it while Gregorio, my other brother, and I sprawled nearby in the scant shade of an orange tree, sipping the ever-present maté.

Lost in thought, I barely followed their conversation. Suddenly, as if thinking aloud, I burst out, "I'm not happy with this state of affairs. An inner voice is telling me to pack a few things and set out to see America. The years I spent in Chañar, with my dream of doing something for the lepers, quelled my desire to seek new horizons. But now that I've been transferred from a place I loved, and where I was loved, and sent to a hospital where everything is cold and calculating, where first they ask whether a patient can pay for tests and only later whether he needs them or not, I need broader horizons."

"That's easy," Tomás interrupted, "just get Ernesto on the back and go like this—" and he imitated the noise of the bike at top speed.

I said nothing but took the maté from Gregorio, who

was constantly preparing it. As I sipped, I said to myself: Why not? What better time than this to put the plan into action? I've the energy and desire. What more do I need?

The rasping sound of the empty maté gourd interrupted my train of thought and, handing it back to Gregorio, I exclaimed, "Right, gentlemen, before this year ends, the journey's on."

That night over dinner I told my parents. They knew that this time I meant it, and instead of their usual pleasant reaction there was a strange heavy silence.

Later, tossing and turning in bed, I wondered whether I could do it. Would the unspoken disapproval of family and friends dissuade me? Would the sense of fulfillment outweigh the suffering I was about to cause them? I knew that in realizing my deep desire, the joy of achieving it would make up for the pain of parting.

Suddenly I had another worry. Would Pelao agree to come? Was it not madness to expect him to travel when he was so close to finishing his medical degree? Was it not wrong of me to take him away from Dr. Pisani, when Ernesto could no doubt have a brilliant future with him?

Fúser himself provided the answers when he made a surprise visit to Córdoba to see his girlfriend Chichina. The moment I told him my plan, he said he didn't give a shit about the future I saw for him with a doctor who, though brilliant, was trapped in the confines of the medical trade. And with that, Ernesto flung himself into a war dance, whooping and yelling, and the pact between us was sealed.

The next days were a mad whirl of maps, spare parts and dozens of routes adopted and abandoned in turn. Finally, despite my parents' silent opposition—and the less silent opposition of aunts and uncles, who considered the trip utterly mad—the big day arrived.

The bike looked like a huge prehistoric animal. On either side were waterproof canvas bags and on the back a rack loaded with everything from a grill for barbecuing meat to a tent and camp beds.

Our chosen route was as follows: we would head south to Buenos Aires so that Fúser could say goodbye to his mother and father, and then we'd go down the Atlantic coast as far as Bahía Blanca. From there we'd cross the provinces of La Pampa and Neuquén to see the southern lakes and then make our way over the Andes. Once in Chile, we'd head north to Caracas.

Everybody was nervous and excited. Surrounded by a noisy swarm of children, attracted by the look of the bike and the odd way we were dressed, we began our farewells. After taking a few snapshots "for posterity," I embraced my parents, who choked back their emotion, and my brothers, who watched us with affectionate envy. I kissed my mother one last time, grateful for the effort she made not to cry. Without more ado, I started the engine. Ernesto climbed onto the back and off we went, wobbling under the burden of luggage. Pelao turned to wave, and for a moment his sudden movement made me lose control of the bike. We almost crashed into a tram that was coming round the corner. The cries of alarm that went up told me how great our danger had been. To avoid any further delay—and in spite of protests and thumps on the back from Pelao—I accelerated, my eyes straight ahead, until we were lost in the traffic and my family's and friends' affectionate anxiety lay far behind. Ahead lay excitement and new horizons.

Villa Gesell, 6 January 1952
I've seen the sea at last! And just the way I wanted to see it for the first time: at night, by moonlight.

I'm overlooking the vast Atlantic, propped against the dunes and gazing at the beach and the waves. Only nine days into the journey, and already I can tell by what we've

seen, learned and been through how wonderful and important this trip—finally a reality—will be for our futures.

But back to the 29th. Having narrowly avoided hitting
the tram, I rode away at full speed and only after hurtling
along at a dizzying speed for twenty or thirty blocks pulled
over to the curb. Ernesto was furious.

"You shit, Mial!" he said, catching his breath. "I had to
hang on like an octopus!"

Fúser's anger was comic and made me burst into nervous laughter. After we'd both had a laugh, I explained the
obvious. "If I'd stopped, the fuss would have welded us to
our maternal hearths for ever."

After sorting ourselves out we set off again. We had a
few problems, all caused by the luggage—including a fall
that damaged the accumulator—but eventually we got to
the town of Ballesteros, groping along in the dark. There,
under the eaves of a humble farmhouse, we tended to the
bike and after a few matés got into our sleeping bags. As I
lay savoring the joys of my first night as a transcontinen-
tal trekker, weariness immediately overcame me and
sleep interrupted my ramblings.

The stretch from Ballesteros to Rosario went quickly
and without incident. Here we spent some time with my
nieces, who were all impressed by Fúser's intelligence and
good looks. Our aspirations, however, are a long way from
their dreams, inspired by radio soaps and a cheap women's
magazine like *Vosotras*.

We reached Buenos Aires where, as at my home, we
were subjected to cutting remarks about our famous trip
and its likelihood of failure. We had to listen to the usual
drivel about how we should follow the well-trodden path
that Fúser's family had followed. Only his mother was not
negative. All she said was, "Alberto, you're the elder, so
I'm asking you, try to get Ernesto to come back and finish
his studies. A degree never hurts."

On 4 January we set out for the Atlantic coast. We went through Palermo Park. As usual there were people selling all sorts of different breeds of dogs by the roadside. Pelao wanted to give Chichina a present when we saw her in Miramar, where she was spending the summer, and, falling in love with an Alsatian puppy, he bought it. He named it, in English, Come Back—no doubt as some sort of promise to Chichina.

After we'd gone a few miles along the Mar del Plata highway, a torrential downpour hit us. We had to turn off and head for a dairy farm about half a mile away. When the storm passed, we continued east. But this stretch, over mud, alerted us to the dangers of dirt roads, so different from the terrain around Córdoba or the salt flats we were used to. We spent that night by the side of the road in a police sentry box. The next day, after waiting for Come Back to have his breakfast (he could only drink milk), we continued on our way to Villa Gesell, a spot almost unknown to the typical tourist. It's very pretty, with simple bungalows, broad beaches and a great surf that comes sweeping in smoothly to the shore.

Miramar, 13 January 1952

We reached this beautiful beach seven days ago. Our stay here has been an eye-opener. I've met a lot of people from a social class I've never encountered before, and frankly it makes me proud of my origins. I had never come across the upper class before, let alone socialized with them. It's incredible the way they think, the way they reason. Here are people who believe that it is their divine right—or something of the kind—to live without a care in the world, except for their social standing, or wasting time together in the stupidest possible ways. Fortunately, Chichina in particular and the Guevaras in general (especially Fúser's sister Ana María) are nothing like them.

I talked this over with Pelao. "Listen, mate, these people make me feel better about myself. We at least have created something—a rugby team, a research lab. We've fed our intellects, while these characters—with all the possibilities open to them, with every advantage—squander all their energy on pointless activities, purely for their own pleasure. No wonder they're astonished when they hear you talk about equality, or when you point out that others have to live too. All those around them, who serve them, who clean up after them, these are people too; they too would like to bathe in the sea and enjoy the sun."

On the 11th, after dark, I went down to the shore. It was unforgettable. There were two different landscapes. By the sea the dunes sloped smoothly down to the beach, where the breaking waves formed a wall of white foam. On the other side was a lunar landscape made up of hillocks, like craters surrounding small ponds with a few silvery shrubs reflected in their moonlit waters. It was marvelous!

What puzzles me is how all these people, who talked about how deeply they felt the beauty of the night and the place, didn't share my great desire that everyone in the world should be able to admire and enjoy such beauty.

Today we went swimming. When we got out of the water we joined the group of visitors spending their holidays with Ernesto's aunt and Chichina. Several of them are university students. A discussion soon started about political and social questions. We discussed the recent nationalization of healthcare by the Labour government in England. Ernesto held forth and for almost an hour he warmly defended nationalization, but condemned the abuse of medicine for profit, the uneven distribution of urban and rural doctors, the scientific isolation of country doctors, who then lapse into commerce, and spoke on many other subjects.

I was a few feet away from those who were talking and

couldn't help feeling the affection and admiration I have always had for Pelao. First off, he comes from the same background as the others, yet the views of his class have not dulled his sensitivity. Not only that—he takes a stance against all that they accept as natural. Listening to his solid arguments and the scathing ripostes with which he made nonsense of their feeble rebuttals, I thought: This Pelao reveals a new side every day. He and I had been over this ground many times before, but how well he was putting his points across today!

After demolishing his opponents, Fúser turned to me, grabbed Come Back and said, "Let's shake off these guys, Petiso (Shorty), and go bathe the dog." We dashed across the sand away from the group, who went on talking and perhaps wondering at Pelao's dialectics.

As I always say—you can hate or admire Ernesto, but you can never ignore him.

Necochea, 14 January 1952

Today we're on our way again. We're at Tamargo's—he and I were at university together for five years. We were both involved in the student struggle of 1943. A bunch of us rented a house near the university hospital, played sports together, clashed with police thugs and helped democratize the Córdoba Students' Union. We left university only four years ago, but how we've grown apart! We no longer understand each other. Tamargo has treated us well, I can't deny that—once, that is, he got over the shock of my turning up on a noisy motorbike, covered in grease and dust.

It drives me to despair that a young man whose outlook until a few years ago was progressive should become completely absorbed by the loathsome society around him. He knows that all this is wrong, that he's charging more for lab tests than they're worth, but still he does it and even seems to take morbid pleasure in going against the dictates of his conscience. He's already a fossil, with his pretty house and lady wife, with her small-town, middle-class mentality, her only concern that everything be in its place and spotless. It is. But it's also devoid of ideas and generous feelings.

Bahía Blanca, 16 January 1952

We arrived in Bahía Blanca, at the home of some friends of Ernesto's—the Saravias, who treated us lavishly. We then went all the way to Necochea in one go, stopping in the shade of two weeping willows in Río Quequén Salado to barbecue a strip of ribs, which did us for both breakfast and lunch. We had to adjust the valves, as the strong wind was making the bike misfire. This is the first little fondle we've given "Poderosa II" in almost 1,200 miles.

The pampa of the Ranqueles[1]

Benjamin Zorrilla, 23 January 1952

After seven days I'm returning to my poor abandoned diary.

We spent three days getting the bike ready. We traveled through Bahía Blanca and Puerto White, trying without much luck to change the few pesos we had into Chilean or Peruvian currency. We got about 200 Chilean pesos and 100 dollars for 1,100 Argentine pesos. We've got about 2,000 pesos left, which we'll have to change in Bariloche, where tourists go. We received a warm welcome from the Saravias. The most picturesque event was a chance acquaintance with some office clerk who offered to show us the city's nightlife. It was a boring evening. Listening to his paeans of self-praise, his descriptions of amorous conquests, the great deals he was about to clinch, and seeing how he lived his whole life wrapped up in himself, we realized that none of our irony and sometimes open mockery was getting through to him. Afterward Fúser and I remarked that this was pretty much what our futures would have been—me a small-town pharmacist, he a doctor treating the allergies of wealthy ladies—if it weren't for that certain something that made us rebel.

On the 21st, before we left Bahía Blanca, locals warned us that crossing the dunes would present difficulties. You

[1] The Ranqueles are an Indian nation who around 1775 settled in the Argentine provinces of San Luis, Córdoba, Santa Fe and Buenos Aires. They originally came from the foot of the Andes.

had to set out at dawn when the sand was coated with dew. Naturally, we set out at midday, when the bike was ready. We were not about to wait around another day. The sand felt as if it was on fire. We had twelve spills, each more spectacular than the last. After Médanos, Fúser drove. We took another dramatic tumble when we hit a dune at high speed, but the knock did no great damage.

It rained quite heavily at dusk and we had to ask for shelter in a shack. We stayed till dawn. On the 22nd we were on the road to Choele Choel. The route was much like the one linking Simbolar and Rayo Cortado in the Córdoba mountains, which I remember from my journeys from the leprosarium to Córdoba and back. At midday, aching all over from the miles and miles we had covered on a rough, bumpy highway, we stopped at the picturesque little town of Pichi Mahuida, on the bank of the Colorado River.

We barbecued some meat in the shade of a pine copse that grew almost down to the river bank of reddish sand. This was the prettiest spot we've camped in so far. After eating, we set off for Choele Choel, but the bike started having carburetor trouble and we ran out of fuel. We had to wait for a vehicle to come past and ask for some petrol. That's how we got to the railway station at Zorrilla. We were given permission to sleep in a shed for storing wheat. Now we're drinking maté with the watchman and getting ready to leave for Fort General Roca.

Today we had the worst setback of the journey so far. Fúser's asthma had been giving him trouble since he woke up. Shortly after I'd finished writing the above, he began to shiver as if feverish. He felt nauseated, lay down and vomited bile. He ate nothing all day. Right now we're preparing to leave for Choele Choel, where there's a first-aid center.

Choele Choel, 25 January 1952

As I write, thinking back to the day before yesterday, everything seems a distant bad dream. We set out from Zorrilla at about seven o'clock, just as the sun was setting, and drove slowly so that the bike wouldn't jolt so much, as Pelao had a splitting headache. We got to the first-aid center, really a regional hospital, and were seen by a male nurse. He was very rude to us and sent us to speak to the director, who lives several blocks away. We introduced ourselves—Ernesto as a medical student and myself as a biochemist—in view of which he sent us back with a note. When the nurse learned that we held the rank of doctor and "almost doctor," there was a radical change in his behavior. Instead of a corner in the garage, which is where he had first thought of putting us up, he gave us a room with two beds and an adjoining bathroom. In other words, we'd turned into two gentlemen instead of a pair of tramps—as if having a degree made us more sensitive to cold or comforts than two humble workers would have been.

Yesterday afternoon Ernesto's fever had almost broken, so I went out for a stroll through Choele. I crossed the bridge over the Río Negro and, leaning against the parapet, let my imagination wander. First I thought about home. Then I considered the possibility that the five of us might one day travel to Europe—across Spain, through central Europe, see the Danube and the USSR and hear the bells of the Kremlin, just as I had told my friend Corcho González I would, when we were in jail in 1943.

Then I went on as far as the allotments on the outskirts of town. I felt happy, for nothing makes a person happier than to see his dreams come true. I thought of all those to whom I had confided my plans when they were still fantasies—especially the girls, for whom the trip was their most dreaded rival: Tomasita and Pirincha, in Villa

Concepción; Negra, Delfina and Turca, in Chañar; and dozens of others, who were still leading dull lives, but happy to do so. My life had been no different, but I always considered I was marking time. My new life had now begun, but I have no regrets about the old one.

I strolled cheerfully on and came upon reedy marshes. Among the thickets I saw scampering creatures that looked like tiny marsupials, inhabitants of some mysterious, still undiscovered world, but they were only coots embellished by my imagination.

The allotments had been flattened by hail a few days earlier. Unripe apples and pears covered the grass. I bought a few peaches from one of the gardeners to share with Fúser. I got a lift back from the driver of a small truck and within minutes I was at the hospital again. I had supper, left the peaches for Ernesto, who was asleep, and went off to write.

Chichinales, 27 January 1952

We set off yesterday with restored health and damaged pockets. At midday, after passing through a number of towns with Indian names—Chelforé, Quequén, etc.—we reached Chichinales. Place names are all that are left of that indomitable race since armies of gauchos were sent out by Buenos Aires, Paris and London to "civilize the desert" and, while they were about it, kill the Indians and steal their land.

After various delays owing to punctures we reached Cipolletti, one of the principal towns in the province of Neuquén. Technology and man's industry begin to show a few miles before you reach the place. The rivers have been channeled, and the once-barren land is fertile and rich. Instead of scrub there are fruit trees and acre upon acre of vineyards.

After various vain attempts, we managed to get permission to sleep in an empty cell in the police station. In the cell next to ours were two prisoners sitting down to a sumptuous dinner. They were a couple of speculators being held temporarily and, in exchange for a few bottles of wine—a pittance to them—they had reduced the poor police constables to a state of abject servitude.

This is only logical, since the fine that these crooks calling themselves traders have been forced to pay only goes from the small coffers it was in before to the big ones of four or five upstarts who hold office, and from there to the coffers of the national oligarchy or the foreign banks. These last are the ones who profiteer, as always, from the money made by the efforts of ordinary people. This money ought to go to increase the national budget so that the country can educate the people, who know only the beauties of alcohol, soccer and horse racing. They have been led in this direction for centuries by classroom, pulpit and press, which are all in the hands of the rich and powerful. The people have been deprived of every opportunity to discover their own power, for this would incite them to rebellion and increase their desire to live a better life.

As I was discussing this with Ernesto, he surprised me once more with one of his pithy expressions. "Petiso," he said to me, talking to himself, "this is how it is. Heads and tails, always the two sides of the coin. The beauty of the landscape and the natural wealth of the land set against the poverty of those who work it. The nobility and generosity of the poor set against the mean and sordid spirits of the landowners and of those who rule the country."

His words stuck firmly in my mind, and as I slept amidst the din of the crooked speculators, who were already half drunk, I seemed to hear Fúser's voice echoing and re-echoing: heads and tails, heads and tails, heads and tails.

En route to Piedra del Aguila, 28 January 1952

We set out from Cipolletti at nine in the morning. We bought supplies in the city of Neuquén, then went on as far as the Cabo Alarcón estancia, where we had lunch. As we got under way again a furious south wind began to blow, lashing us mercilessly. The road is rough and the landscape too. Bare hills alternate with plains of stunted scrub and an immense solitude. Miles and miles without even glimpsing a house, an animal—or anything. As I was driving I thought: We know that after this stretch of desert road, the beauty of the Andean lakes awaits us, but what must it have been like for those early pioneers, who traveled without knowing when or where they would arrive?

My mind on these and other thoughts, we came to Picún Leufú, where we filled up with petrol. Then on we went to Bajada Colorada. The terrain became even more arid still and the wind grew fiercer. It wasn't sand that buffeted our faces now, but tiny stones blown up by the dust devils that pelted our bodies and our goggles. A mile or two before Bajada Colorada the true Andean foothills began, with their steep climbs and abrupt descents.

We arrived in Bajada Colorada and went to a branch of the Argentine Automobile Club. The service was abominable, just as in all the others we've been to. We met a group of Chilean rally drivers. They all complained about the poor service they'd received from this organization supported by subscriptions and with a mandate to assist its members. It's a bureaucracy that uses the money collected from members to send its directors on trips abroad and organize races that bring in fat profits, but provides little to those whose monthly payments keep the organization going.

We drove on to Piedra del Aguila. Because of the encroaching hills, darkness came much earlier than on previous days. We found an avenue of trees and turned off, thinking it was the entrance to some sheep ranch. Within half a mile the path petered out in the scrub. We left the bike and continued on foot toward what, in the semi-darkness, we thought was a house. It turned out to be the remains of an old fortlet, called Nogueras, an outpost of the Buenos Aires army in Indian territory. We returned to the bike in deep twilight and got on the road again, lashed by the wind, which seemed even fiercer now after the brief respite of the tree-lined avenue.

A few miles on, driving almost blind, we fell into three consecutive potholes and, as we came out of the last one, I felt myself being pitched forward. The frame of the bike was broken. We struggled feverishly to put up the tent, but the gale prevented us. In the end we leaned the bike against a telegraph pole, tied one end of the tent to it and stretched the canvas out to form a kind of wall to curb the force of the great south wind. We couldn't build a camp fire so close to the bike and the pole, so we piled on all our clothes and got into our respective sleeping bags. Before delivering myself into the arms of Morpheus, I said ironically to Fúser, "This time the coin came down on its edge."

Piedra del Aguila, 29 January 1952
Today, after tying the handlebars with wire to keep them on the bike, we limped into town and had the frame welded. Unable to find lodgings, we asked if they'd let us stay in the garage where we got the bike mended. Squeezed into the grease pit, we're spending our second uncomfortable night of the journey.

En route to San Martín de los Andes, 30 January 1952
We reached the Collón Curá River and crossed it on a ferry that runs along a cable, which keeps the swift current from sweeping it downstream.

After traveling on a few miles we found a path leading to an estancia. We went in to try and buy some meat for lunch. Sheer coincidence had brought us to this place, where we found evidence that German junkers—Nazis, of course—have penetrated into Patagonia. There had been talk about this during the early years of the Second World War, but then it was kept quiet. The owner is a fairly young German who looks like a Prussian officer. His surname says it all—Von Puttkammer.[2]

The main house is an imitation Black Forest structure. They've even introduced deer, which over the years have adapted and bred. We looked over as much of the estate as we could manage, as it is absolutely vast. The Chimehuin River, which flows through it, is a typical mountain river—rushing, deep and crystal-clear, with dozens of rainbow trout.

We forgot about the German and all our conjectures, and threw ourselves into the magic of fishing. One of the hands lent us some gear and we caught a number of trout. Along the way we came upon a ripe cherry orchard. Pelao ate a handful, but I made such a pig of myself that I couldn't eat either the fish or ribs that Fúser grilled and that smelled so wonderful. I had to resign myself to spending all that night and part of the next day with the runs.

On the shore of Lake Nahuel Huapí, 8 February 1952

It's about eight o'clock in the evening. A week ago at this time we were making our entry into San Martín de los Andes and now here we are by the lake some sixty miles from Bariloche. Until a few moments ago, the Nahuel Huapí was a beautiful shade of blue. Now that the sun is setting the lake has become a rippling silvery surface. Beyond the lake, the Andes rise majestically, veiled in a

---

[2] In fact the Von Puttkammer family claims to have been established in Argentina long before the Second World War.

bluish mist that heightens their beauty. As I watch the sun disappear between two snowy peaks, I'm making an effort to write down every detail of what's happened to us in the past week. For me, even the smallest things have been crucial.

On Thursday the 31st we slept in a National Park shed in San Martín de los Andes. We met the park ranger, a friendly guy who's very concerned about the conservation of flora and fauna. We also met Don Olate, the night watchman, who was the stuff of folk songs. A typical gaucho, he weighs over 300 pounds and has a job getting about. Fond of conversation and red wine, he was very eager for us to stay on. We slept there. At dawn, we set out with a knapsack of provisions to see Lake Lacar. It's completely surrounded by mountains, their slopes covered with huge trees. I was struck by the primitive beauty and serenity of the place.

As we sat drinking maté by the lake, Pelao and I dreamed up a medical research lab with a helicopter to fetch supplies every morning. Snapping out of our reverie, we went back to the shed and accepted the night watchman's job offer to help him prepare a roast lamb for a lunch given by the Automobile Club to a group of racing drivers. We spent the whole morning hauling firewood, building a fire, raising and lowering the spit under Don Olate's expert eye. Just as we expected, he dumped all the work on us, but we greatly enjoyed it.

We kept trying the roast, again and again, washing each tidbit down with plenty of wine. This gave us the bright idea of pinching three of the many bottles available. Fúser played drunk, and we wandered off with the wine under our shirts, hiding the bottles in a hollow by the road. Feeling quite smug, we chatted with a new character, Don Pendón, who was a perfect hermaphrodite. He was a man, but everything about him—his voice, hair, breasts and the way he walked—was that of a woman. He must have more Xs in his chromosomes than a mathematics textbook.

During our conversation we mentioned that we came from Córdoba, and he told us he worked for a construction company that employed several men from Córdoba, among them a certain Luis Loyola. "He's from Villa Concepción del Tío[3] and he's a friend of mine," I said. "If you see him, tell him Granado's here."

By now it was night. We collected the remains of the lamb for our supper, taking our time until everyone had left. Then, very pleased with ourselves, we went to fetch the bottles. But they were gone.

On the 3rd we went to see the motor races, since our good work at the spit had earned us two tickets. It was a boring spectacle. As we were on our way back we were stopped by a jeep. It was Don Pendón, bringing Luis Loyola.

After the obligatory embraces and questions we went to a bar where Tomasito León, Horacio Cornejo and Alfredo Moriconi—all old friends from Villa Concepción del Tío—were waiting for us. They were overjoyed to see me, and I felt very moved and happy. At once we began drinking to each other's health, and decided to go to Junín de los Andes, where they live. We left the tent and camp beds there in San Martín and set out, they in the jeep, we on the bike. At their place we ate like horses and slept like logs. The next day they took us to the site where they worked. With an arc welder, they welded the bike's frame all over again.

That night we barbecued a lamb, amply washed down with a fine local wine. It was all very good, but what really made it special for me was the affection of my old friends and their eagerness to wine and dine us in such style. We remembered the dances and picnics I used to

[3] Villa Concepción del Tío: a small town in the province of Córdoba where the author lived and worked as a pharmacist from May 1946 to April 1947.

organize, which, according to them, never took place again. All my amorous conquests were aired—Tomasita, Pirincha, Liebre and Gorda, Tristán and Horacio's sister. In short, it seemed I'd had more adventures than Casanova.

As a brother of one of my supposed conquests was present, I changed the subject, and we went on eating and drinking. In honor of the old days, we went and performed an a capella serenade for Horacio's wife, the mother of two little Cornejos. We woke her and continued the party at their house until the sun came up. We got up late, with hangovers, and couldn't set out that day, so another farewell dinner was organized, at the end of which they brought out champagne. Pelao was amazed at how fondly I was remembered in that town. So was I.

On the 6th, after mutual promises that we would meet in Villa Concepción del Tío on some future 8 December, the day of the town's patron saint, we started back to San Martín de los Andes.

The sandy road was bad, which forced us to drive slowly, yet we still fell several times, though without hurting ourselves. Soon both the road and the landscape began to improve. A corniche road as picturesque as it was dangerous took us along beside Lake Carhué Chico and then to Lake Carhué Grande a few miles further on. The latter is a very beautiful spot, surrounded by high mountain peaks, many of which are permanently snow-capped. There and then we decided to climb one of them. We came to a forest ranger's cabin and asked him to look after the bike. We bought a couple of loaves of bread from him and began our ascent.

We followed a stream that flows into the lake. Its course was completely choked with fallen trees—giant copihues, lengas, oaks and ashes. The water snaked between and over the top of tree-trunks felled by lightning and wind.

The slope grew steeper and steeper, and the stream began to turn into ever larger waterfalls. At one we had to leave the course of the stream and plunge into a thick reed-bed shaded by huge trees.

After four hours of hard climbing, we reached the wooded part of the peak and turned off toward a crag that rose before us, seemingly impregnable. We struggled up on all fours, clinging to boulders and taking advantage of anything we could get a grip on.

A few yards from the snowfield that crowned the summit, Ernesto, who was leading the way, took hold of an outcrop, only to have it break away. He tried desperately to prop it up, since, if it fell, it would drag him down with it. I rushed to his side and took part of the weight with one hand, but without a firm foothold we both ran the risk of being dragged down. With great effort we moved apart, he to the left and I to the right, and we let the boulder slide between us. It was only when I saw it go crashing and leaping down and smash to pieces a hundred yards below that I realized what danger we'd been in.

After a brief rest we set out again and soon were gazing in delight at the immense landscape spread out at our feet. We chucked a few snowballs at each other and, after we'd taken three or four photos, we began the descent.

We were pleased with our success, but had no idea of the danger that lay ahead before this little adventure was to come to a close. We started down along the stream formed by the melt-water, clutching the branches of arrayanes, which at this altitude grow like shrubs. The branches were so thick we almost had to crawl under them between the slope and the abyss that opened at our feet.

Our descent became slower and slower. The sun was already going down when we suddenly found ourselves at the edge of a sheer cliff. We faced the choice of either turning back—which would have been suicidal—or trying to pull ourselves up the mountainside by the branches of the coligües, until we found another path. Fúser led the way.

A few yards higher up he came upon a narrow track that went deep into the woods farther down the slope. Climbing after him, I felt the rock supporting the tip of my boot come away. I desperately seized some shrubs growing in the cracks in the rock-face, watching in anguish as their feeble roots came away under my weight. Fortunately my feet found a chink, and I got my fingers into another, so I could hold myself there and catch my breath. Just then, Fúser, who had gone on ahead when he saw me coming, turned round, sensing something odd about my delay. He gave me a hand from above. Panting, I turned back and saw my goggles, which had fallen off during my struggle. The sun's last rays played on them at the bottom of the abyss. They winked at me as if to say, "You just made it by the skin of your teeth."

We continued our descent through the woods and the reed-beds, now shrouded in darkness. Stumbling into fallen trunks, we fell, got up, only to fall once more. We were tired, but one thing was sure—our spirits were high, cracking jokes each time we fell or when our clothes snagged on the scrub. At last, when we found the stream again, it was close to eleven o'clock. We followed its course and shortly afterward we were faced with the marvelous spectacle of the moonlit lake. Although we longed to get back, we had to sit at the edge of the wood and admire the beauty of the lake and the surrounding hills. At that moment, silvered by the moonlight, the woods looked like a petrified forest. At last we reached the forest ranger's cabin. We slept in the kitchen.

The next morning we drove along the shore of Lake Lolog and reached San Martín de los Andes. We loaded our gear and left. We drove past Lake Macheuco and then

skirted Lake Villarino, Lake Hermoso and Lake
Tormentoso. In the end, we decided to stop and camp at
the next lake we came to. A few miles on we found ourselves face to face with Lake Espejo Grande. Impossible to
describe its beauty and serenity, the name says it all: Great
Mirror. We had a funny experience here, which once more
demonstrated Ernesto's capacity to take decisive action on
the spur of the moment.

We camped under a flowering arrayán that almost
touched the water. We ate some tinned meat and decided
to fill the rest of our empty stomachs with maté and stale
bread.

Suddenly a man appeared on foot. He came over and
greeted us. We invited him to sit down and drink maté
with us. He accepted and launched into a long conversation that was sometimes dialogue, sometimes monologue.
He began by extolling the virtues of the bike, asking us
how much it cost and what its cylinder capacity was.
Then he focused his attention on our saddlebags and later
on the quality of our leather jackets.

He did most of the talking, and I answered drily so as
not to encourage his verbal diarrhea. Fúser said nothing
and brewed the maté. Our visitor began to talk about a
Chilean thief who was prowling the area. He warned us
against the dangers of sleeping outdoors with such a man
about, who could easily strip us of bike, clothes and
money. I made a seemingly appropriate remark. Fúser,
mute as the Sphinx, went on brewing maté and watched a
pair of courting ducks that were swimming close to the
shore.

The guy went on and on about the Chilean and tried to
get a few words out of Pelao. Suddenly, in a moment of
silence, Ernesto drew the Smith & Wesson he carried in
the leg of his boot and—almost without aiming—shot at
one of the ducks, which uttered a squawk and lay floating

on its side. Startled, our inopportune visitor leaped to his feet, dropped his maté and bade us a hasty farewell. As he left, Fúser roared with laughter.

Not wanting to put the tent up for just one night, we slept beside the bike with the canvas drawn over us. At dawn we set out for Bariloche. After an eleven-hour drive we ended up looking at the famous Nahuel Huapí, where we are now.

To try and describe it would just be to repeat all the clichés. How to put into words the changing colors of the water and sky, the immensity of the snowy peaks, and the serenity of the whole landscape? All I can say is that once again, without a word to each other, we turned off the road and drove almost to the water's edge. There we sat in the dying rays of the sun and gazed in admiration at the grandeur before us. In the end, the flames of our campfire were all that lit the shore. In its faint light we could just make out the flowery crown of the arrayán beneath which we were camped.

ROOSEVELT HIGH SCHOOL

The perfect exploitation machine

En route to Bariloche, 9 February 1952

Today we had some mechanical setbacks and only covered twenty-five of the sixty remaining miles to Bariloche. We wasted the whole day, but what we've seen and heard in these twenty-four hours was well worth the lost time.

To work on the bike we pushed it to a group of humble dwellings to one side of the road. We soon met a few of the inhabitants, and quickly realized that they were not from around here, but from Santiago and La Rioja—that is, from provinces almost 1,200 miles away.

Intrigued, we gradually worked the conversation round to what brought them here. And this is how we found out about a terrible form of exploitation perpetrated by the Argentine, German, Jewish and Yankee landowners of this extremely wealthy agricultural region.

This is a vast area of over 100,000 square miles, whose rich natural grazing and small woodlands allow for vast sheep-farming operations, practically without the need for human labor. Each rancher has two or three farm hands scattered about his land, and they and their families cover great distances on horseback, keeping an eye on the occasional injured animal or ewe having trouble lambing— only minor things, because these oligarchs are as crafty as they are callous. They have even exterminated the red fox, the only wild animal to prey on young sheep, by offering a bounty of one Argentine peso for every male fox killed and five for every female. Fifteen years ago, five pesos were a week's wages for a farm hand. Within a few years the females were exterminated and the species practically wiped out. That is to say, the landowners' wealth increased without their having to invest in equipment, employees or farm hands.

But there is one time of the year when they do need numbers of workers—the shearing season. So once again the perfect exploitation machine swings into action. Hundreds of flyers are printed offering shearers work, board and good wages. These leaflets are distributed around Chubút, Neuquén, the southern part of the province of Buenos Aires, Córdoba, Mendoza, and even as far afield as Santiago del Estero, San Juan and La Rioja. The local workers, who know all about the trick, don't fall for it, but the unemployed from other provinces arrive in numbers, on their own or with their families. Their ranks are swollen by hundreds of Chileans, also driven by hunger. It's at moments like this that the true face of capitalism is revealed.

Five hundred or more shearers arrive at a ranch where 300 are needed. So the boss, making a mockery of trade-union legislation, starts an auction. Instead of uniting and saying, "Nobody shears any cheaper; let the sheep keep their wool," the laborers feel forced to enter into shady deals and end up working for a much lower wage. In some cases—like those of the people we were talking to—the workers do not return to their native provinces after the shearing season, but take jobs here and there in an attempt to be the first ones at the next shearing.

As we gradually learned about this exploitation and the men's utter poverty, the injustice of it filled us with hatred. But this isn't all. When we asked where the flocks were, they said along the rivers. This allows the owners to transport their wool by boat to ports from where it is shipped to European markets.

The plundering could not be more perfect. The land-owners don't need to take care of or improve the land, for they have millions and millions of acres. They don't need to invest in wages, for there are thousands of unemployed hands about. They don't need to build roads, for the rivers themselves serve as highways, and the wool goes directly to foreign capitals, where the owners play polo and drive Alfa Romeos and Bugattis. All Argentina gets is exploitation of its people and depletion of its flora and fauna.

"You're right, Ernesto, heads and tails. People and countries impoverished and exploited for the comfort of domestic and foreign capitalists."

Bariloche, 11 February 1952
Yesterday we had another day of ups and downs that ended in a tragicomic incident.

After saying goodbye to the laborers, we set out for nearby—but hard-to-reach—Bariloche. A few miles along the way, the bike's chain came off as we were starting up a hill. We spent several hours trying to mend it, but to no avail. Around midday a little gaucho of about ten, riding on a beautiful pony, told us that the ranch where he worked as assistant to the polo groom was half a mile away at the crest of the rise.

I went as far as the house on foot and asked permission to take the bike there. It was granted. This permission was given by a woman who either owned or was in charge of the ranch. She had a beautiful fox terrier, which kept close to her the whole time we were chatting and growled at frequent intervals.

We pushed the bike up the hill, which was so steep it took a superhuman effort. There were moments in our exhaustion when it didn't seem we could budge the bike.

Once we had conquered the hill, we leaned "Poderosa II" against a pile of straw and sat for a long while recovering our strength.

Then we built a camp fire and had a few matés while we chatted with several of the farm hands under the constant watchful eye of the fox terrier, which barked at us every time we made a move toward the bike. As we were replacing a few links in the chain with others from a tractor, the conversation turned to a subject we'd heard mentioned before—the presence of a Chilean puma (we never did find out how they could tell it from an Argentine puma), which was a nightmare to all the watchmen round the borders of the estancia.

We tried out the bike. The patched-up chain worked. Then we went to eat as the guests of the farm hands. As ever, poor people are more generous and hospitable than rich estate owners.

When night fell we climbed into the hayloft and fell asleep on the spot, utterly worn out by the day's exertions. Suddenly we were awakened by a strange noise. Above the doorway, we saw two eyes glowing in the dark. Still half asleep I heard a shot fired by Ernesto, who—quick and timely as ever—had taken his revolver out of the satchel he was using as a pillow. Immediately after, we heard a howl and I said, "You fucked that puma, Pelao," and we went back to sleep.

We were woken at dawn by cries of grief from the owner of the ranch. She had just found her dog lying rigid, a bullet in its head. She was in such a rage that it was no good trying to explain to her what had happened. She hurled a stream of insults at us, interrupting herself only to cry, "My poor little dog."

Without further ado we gathered up our things, and as we couldn't get the bike to start we jumped onto it and plunged down the hill, pursued by the insults and lamentations of the poor woman, who clasped her dead dog in her arms.

When we got to Bariloche today, after wandering about a bit we managed to get ourselves fixed up for the night at the barracks of the National Guard—an army corps intended to protect the borders from smuggling, but in fact used as an instrument of repression by whatever government is in office. To all appearances it is separate from the Argentine army, but of course—like the army—it obeys only the policies of the ruling oligarchy and their foreign masters.

That night we ate dinner with the group on duty. A sailor was eating with them too. He had jumped ship in Calcutta and was being taken under guard to Buenos Aires via Chile. He painted a vivid picture of his adventures on board a privateer under Panamanian colors sailing the Caribbean coasts, and of the long monotony of the voyage from the Panama Canal to the coast of China. He described the squalid life in the port of Hong Kong, whose starving inhabitants wait on their junks for leftover refuse to be thrown from visiting ships and then hurl themselves like gulls to fight over every scrap.

Bariloche, 12 February 1952

This afternoon we met a couple from New Jersey in their sixties who have driven here from the United States in a station wagon. Although the vehicle is well equipped, it's still admirable that they should have the spirit and energy to undertake such a journey at their age. We arranged to have dinner together tonight when they got back from a drive along the shores of the lake.

We waited a long while, and far past the time we'd agreed to meet Pelao and I returned sad and hungry to the police station, where the prisoners were just being fed. So we had dinner in the most picturesque and select company imaginable.

We stood round the table gnawing a chunk of cold meat. Those sharing our banquet were, opposite me, the sailor who had deserted, who was bragging—without ceasing to chew—that although he was eating this rubbish now, in former days, in Japan, he had bought a fourteen-year-old girl for his personal use and later given her away; to my left, a hardened criminal, who was eating ceremoniously and in silence; a drunk who was so awash with alcohol that he could no longer eat and was jabbering unintelligibly; and opposite, striking a delicate note by virtue of her femininity, an unfortunate madwoman who mumbled obscenities as she ate. We finished quickly and left the Dantesque scene, which was a faithful reflection of the ravaged state to which human beings are brought when we do not stand up to the vile, corrupt system that rules us.

In Araucania

Yesterday we crossed the imaginary but real line that separates Argentina from Chile. I can't say that, in the words of the pasodoble, "I turned back, my eyes full of tears," because although I was leaving my motherland and loved ones behind, there were others to love and new countries to see as our compass pointed north to the rest of Latin America.

If anything saddened us it was that we clearly witnessed, yet again, as in so many other parts of our beloved Argentina, the need for a radical sociopolitical change that would end man's exploitation of man and the exploitation of our country by international cartels.

In the morning we put "Poderosa II" aboard the launch that crosses Lake Nahuel Huapí and were soon surrounded by the curious eyes of Yankee, German, Chilean and Argentine tourists, who badgered us with questions and marveled at our audacity. Of course, none of them thinks we'll make it farther than Santiago de Chile, with or without the bike. We shall see what we shall see, I said to myself. Before setting out, we had changed our last pesos into dollars. We'll see how far they stretch.

When we reached Puerto Blest, we went straight on to Puerto Alegre, where another launch took us to Puerto Frías, the last Argentine customs post in the area. Fifteen miles on, we came to Peulla, a small beautiful city beside

Lake Esmeralda, also known as Todos los Santos, whose emerald color rivals that of the precious stone it's named after. Once more we see the two sides of the coin—heads, the beauty of the landscape and kindness of the people; tails, the fact that all this beauty is exploited by the company that owns the hotel, the coaches that bring in the tourists and the yachts that cruise the lake. A company, in short, that owns the whole place and everyone living here, since it is the only source of jobs. Nobody passes this way without leaving a few pesos in the company's pockets. Naturally, we broke with tradition and, instead of heading for the hotel, went straight to the quay. There, after chatting with the caretaker, we slept in a shed among torn yacht sails and tar-covered ropes.

In line with our policy of not paying for anything if we can help it, after several failed attempts we managed to get a job on a launch that was crossing the lake with a cargo of timber and a car. As payment, they let us bring the bike across.

Lake Nahuel Huapí, 15 February 1952

This morning we loaded the somewhat rickety and far-from-seaworthy launch, which gets towed by the little steamer *Esmeralda* that carries the tourists.

We were barely under way before the launch began to dip at the bow. We had to redistribute the cargo and pass some of it over to the *Esmeralda*. As nobody wanted to dive in to pick up the hawser that had been thrown across—I didn't want Fúser to do it because he had the early signs of a serious asthma attack—I had to do it myself. I was winched up into the other boat, where I made friends with two Brazilian girls, one of whom was studying biochemistry. She was amazed to find a colleague under these circumstances.

I got back to the launch by jumping from the steamer's

winch. We really had to put our backs into it to bale out the bilge, which leaks from all sides. The pump barely works, and we emptied it with buckets. I'm worn out and I've snuck off. I sit writing this in the shade of the bridge. From here I can see waves. The wind has changed, and the bike's getting wet. I'll see if I can get a tarpaulin to cover it.

Lautaro, 21 February 1952

We are completely stranded in this little Chilean town. We've had a serious mechanical setback, which once again shows how slim our chances are of continuing with "Poderosa II." Frankly, this was to be expected. We have come all this way in the most precarious condition. The accumulator broke in Ballesteros only sixty miles after we set out, the rear brake has hardly worked since Bahía Blanca, and we've been more or less braking with the gears. Which is to say that we've had the luxury and run the risk of crossing the highest mountain range in the world almost without brakes, since from Junín de los Andes to here the front brake has hardly been working, either. I'm going to continue my account of events since 15 February.

After covering the bike, I went on baling until we reached Petrohué, where we donned our finery right there in the boat. Pelao even had a bath. Then we went to see the Brazilian girls. I took my colleague down to the lake shore. After talking about biochemistry we went on, by mutual consent, to topographical anatomy. I hope I didn't get as far as embryology.

On the morning of the 16th we got an offer to take a van as far as Osorno. Ernesto would drive it while I followed on the bike. The road to the town runs alongside Lake Llanquihue, at the foot of the Osorno volcano. The lava from old eruptions covered stretches of the road, making it a rough ride.

For the first mile or two the landscape is very beautiful. In places the road is narrow and completely shaded by the trees on either side. Once past the lake, the landscape is completely different.

Here the market gardens appear, little farms that grow wheat, which is, of course, sown and cultivated by exploited tenant farmers, while the profiteering owners live like parasites in Osorno or Santiago.

We got to Osorno. After wandering fruitlessly round the barracks of the border police, we ended up at a private hospital owned by an insurance company. We were welcomed by the administrator, who was very polite and obliging, but whose outlook was so childish and illogical that on several occasions we couldn't help laughing. He tried to convince us that every country—particularly Chile— needs to be ruled by a dictator. All his arguments were so disjointed and far-fetched that frankly, what with the way he peppered them with local turns of phrase, he really could have been a character out of a farce. The only serious and dangerous aspect of all this is that the desire for a dictatorship—represented here by the followers of General Ibáñez[1]—is deeply rooted, and not just in minds like his. We found the same conviction in every inch of Chile we've traveled so far. Only Ibáñez can save the country, though no one has any idea how. People believe in him as if he were a godsend, and of course before long another of our neighbor countries is weighed down by strong-arm rule, led by a man who doesn't even have Perón's intelligence.

We left Osorno on the 17th and were held up for several hours by a trivial accident. We lost the screw that holds the chain-guard on. ("Poderosa II" is now showing all her aches and pains.) At nightfall we asked for shelter at a

[1] Carlos Ibáñez del Campo (1877–1960), general and politician, who was twice elected President of Chile, but ruled as a dictator.

small farm. We gave them the broken-headlight story, and they let us stay, even inviting us to dinner. The man who took care of us is a poor tenant farmer. The owner of his land (and of several other small farms) doesn't even allow him a fraction of the harvest. Who is going to set right this kind of injustice? Ibáñez! Fúser and I looked at each other and by tacit agreement we said nothing.

The next day we began rather cautiously to talk about land reform, about how the land ought to belong to those who work it and not to those who sometimes have never even seen it.

The poor man cut us short, saying, "I don't want anybody to give me anything; God made both rich and poor. What I want is to be paid for the work I do, and General Ibáñez will see to that."

We thanked him and left, crestfallen.

We got to Valdivia and went to the Argentine consulate where we got a very poor reception, of course. Having turned up in all our motorcycle gear, covered in grease and dust, the consul—oh so proper, immaculate and upright—took one look and decided we were unworthy of his attention and got rid of us as quickly as possible.

Once we got away we strolled along the wharf on the river Calle-Calle. The seaport of Corrales is ten miles from Valdivia and the only way to get there is by river. Heading nowhere in particular, we passed the offices of the Valdivia daily. We introduced ourselves, and our lives took a new turn. The paper immediately published a two-column article about us, with a series of jaw-droppingly laughable dithyrambs and inaccuracies.

We left for Temuco at about five o'clock in the afternoon. At dusk we came to a big farm called Los Ciruelos. We trotted out the headlight story again; saying it had just broken. As ever we got a cool reception, but when they found out, during the course of the conversation, that we were doctors, things warmed up. Instead of a corner in one of the outbuildings, where they put us at first, we ended up in the guest room after having consumed a good dinner and regaled them with all our adventures.

On the 18th we set out for Temuco. After about twenty-five miles we had a puncture. It was a rotten day. A fine drizzle gradually soaked us to the skin. As we were getting out the tools to change the inner tube, the sun came out in the form of a van whose driver offered us a lift as far as Temuco. We got "Poderosa II" (soon to be renamed "Weakling II") into the back and started to get to know the driver. He turned out to be a veterinary student, with lots of good ideas and a nice personality. We arranged to meet that night and paint the town red.

We got the bike down in a back street, and I got the wheel off while Ernesto went to a nearby house to ask for hot water to brew maté. A maid answered the door and not only gave him the water, but invited him to bring the bike along too. We had just got settled when the caballero, or master of the house, arrived. He was an elderly man, who, owing to his outfit and his long hair, Fúser figured must be some sort of artist or bohemian, and almost certainly someone with left-wing ideas. What a detective Fúser turned out to be! The man's unkempt mane was a wig.

Shortly afterward, alone with the maid, we subjected her to a grilling. She told us that the caballero, as we dubbed him, has twelve wigs and had gone to Buenos Aires expressly to have more made for him. This information fueled plenty of cheap cracks on our part as we sweated to get the damn tire off. The task mostly fell to poor old Pelao, as it did every time a tire needed changing, since he's a lot stronger and handy with this sort of job.

When we'd finished, we went out to look round the town. We happened to bump into a reporter from the

Temuco daily, the *Austral*, who wrote a story about us that included a photo. Naturally in it we stressed our desire to go to Easter Island. Then we went back to sleep at the wigged caballero's place.

The next day we headed north and had another puncture. It didn't seem fair that it should always be Pelao who got stuck with the job, so I dug my heels in and insisted on doing it, which meant that it took longer than it should have. Although it was dusk, we were so anxious to keep going that we drove on in almost total darkness. The road got more and more impassable and, as ill luck would have it, the small farms—which up till then had come one after another—had disappeared. At last, when it was almost pitch-black, we came to a level crossing with a gatekeeper's hut. We asked for lodging and were given the corner of a room. The hut and its inhabitants looked very poor, so we weren't surprised when they offered us only a few matés and a bit of bread. We went to sleep hungry. At seven the next morning, as soon as it was light, we set out for Lautaro.

Before we'd gone a hundred yards I felt myself catapulted forward. I hit the ground and jumped straight up, completely bewildered. Fúser picked himself up too and ran to shut off the petrol. We checked the bike and found the front fork had come loose and, what was more, when the aluminum chassis that protects the gearbox hit the road, it had shattered into four pieces.

More calamities: volunteer firemen

Los Ángeles, 27 February 1952

Here we are in the Los Ángeles Volunteer Firemen's barracks. How did we get here? Fate. I'll go back to the 21st.

Once we'd recovered from the knock, we managed to get to Lautaro. There, after a series of diplomatic maneuvers—and against my better judgement—we decided to get the gearbox welded. It took two days and cost us the last of our cash.

The first day, we were invited to lunch by a petrol-pump attendant from the garage where we left the bike. He's a German who used to live in Paraguay and then settled in Chile. He has a married daughter in Sarandí, in the province of Buenos Aires, and wanted us as an audience— provided all he heard was praise for Argentina. We were delighted.

That night we met up with a crowd of Chileans who were just like the crowd back home. There was the story-teller, the Casanova, one who was the butt of every heavy-handed joke, the tightwad and the spendthrift—in other words, these small towns are just like any small town in Argentina.

We got on with them, and they offered us some wine. We accepted, and after a few glasses we all decided to go to a dance on the wrong side of the tracks. The dance hall was a building on the edge of town. A number of cars and trucks, parked every which way round a dim single-story building, told us this was the place.

We went in and were welcomed by a blast of smoke reeking of alcohol and blended with that unmistakable odor of sweat winning out over perfume. A few drunken couples were dancing to something vaguely resembling a tango. But most of the public was crushed round a zinc counter, where alcoholic drinks—mainly wine—were sold.

We soon met a few familiar faces: a couple of farm hands who had helped us get our broken bike back on the road, and another who, while we waited, had given us a recital on the charango, an instrument made out of the shell of an armadillo. There was also a group of drunks who—thanks to the booze and the tangos—instantly became our nearest and dearest friends.

It wasn't long before the wife of one of them took a fancy to Pelao. Despite his grimy overalls and less-than-aesthetic stubble, being a foreigner and quite good-looking made him coveted prey.

I was already dancing with an Indian woman who was very fond of Argentines and the tango, but who, despite her tastes, wasn't doing much to lead me on. I was thinking about man's capacity to adapt and about his sensory apparatus, when a sudden commotion shook me out of my philosophical musings. The center of attention was Ernesto, who—excited by the atmosphere and the drink—had tried to drag his devoted admirer outside.

She had been agreeable at first, but suddenly changed her mind and began shouting. Her husband came over immediately, armed with a bottle, and was about to hit Fúser from behind. When I saw what was going on, I dropped my partner, ran over to the man and grabbed him from behind. I floored him, or rather—thanks more to the

wine than my blow—he fell. Taking advantage of the confusion, I fled after Pelao, who was already on the run. A
few minutes later, back in our room and still gasping for
breath, Fúser said, "If we go to any more of these dances,
we must solemnly promise not to sweep the women off
their feet."

With the exception of the above-mentioned episode,
our two days in Lautaro were boring and we spent the
whole time dealing with the bike. When we left, the
petrol-pump attendant organized a farewell lunch for us in
the company of several neighborhood girls. They were all
very affectionate. Once again I noted the greater freedom
of Chilean women. The prudishness of the Argentine middle class in keeping an eye on their daughters doesn't exist
here. We left after the meal.

A few miles further on we had another mishap, and I
again witnessed Ernesto's level-headedness and quick
reactions. Once past the built-up area, where I always
drive because I'm the one with the international license, I
turned the bike over to Fúser. As we rounded a bend we
ran into a drove of oxen, and I heard Ernesto call out in a
slightly shaky voice, "The brake's gone!"

We were going downhill and we could see that the slope
ended in a row of poplars some 400 yards ahead. The bike
was still picking up speed, but in fact I felt no fear.
Looking back on it now, knowing that a river ran behind
the poplars, I reckon this could have been the end of the
line for us. At the very least we might have broken a few
bones. But all I did was tell Fúser to brake using the gears
and run the bike into the hill.

With a degree of confidence quite unwarranted in an
inexperienced driver, Ernesto got the bike into third, then
into second, which reduced our speed considerably, and
finally, with difficulty, he got it into first. At once, taking
advantage of our slower speed, he aimed the bike straight

at the bank. As I jumped off the back he spread his legs, and I saw him come off the seat just a fraction of a second before the front wheel hit the mountain. We ran to switch off the engine to prevent a fire, and then shook hands, happy still to be alive.

What had happened was bound to happen. The thread of the wing nut that held the brake lever in place had completely worn away, and the nut had come off. We made our way back to a small farm we had seen a minute or two before. They gave us some wing nuts that we used to patch up the lever, and two hours later we were on our way again.

Owing to our having patched up the gearbox, the bike began to lose power, and as night was coming on we asked for shelter at an hijuela, the local name for a parcel of land smaller than a small farm. We were offered a place in the straw loft. But as the Temuco daily paper had got there ahead of us, one of the owner's daughters knew who we were and whispered something to her father, thanks to which we were invited to dinner. Then they put us up in the guest room.

The next day they gave us a magnificent breakfast, and we left firmly convinced that the press really is the fourth power in a bourgeois republic and that a lot of people believe more in the printed word than in what they see with their own eyes. How dangerous such power can be in unscrupulous hands!

On we went, now struggling against the bike itself as well as the road. Plagued by the strange noises it was making, we stopped at midday on a side road shaded by chestnut trees. There we stripped down the clutch and adjusted the central wing nut.

With the bike running a little better, we started up the hill by the River Malleco, which is spanned by the highest railway bridge in all of South America. Halfway up, the chain snapped. We had to stop right there since we didn't have a spare.

We managed to get a truck driver to give us a lift as far as the little town of Culli Pulli, where a blacksmith was able to mend the chain, but night surprised us in this flurry of activity. A young man who lived nearby offered us a place to sleep, but in exchange we had to listen to a series of tales in which he was either a witness or a protagonist. In each of them there was always at least one dead body.

The next day we tried to carry on, but it was impossible. "Poderosa II" was begging for mercy. We decided to wait for some new truck to give us a lift, which didn't take long. As we drove along we felt a growing desire to leave the bike behind in Santiago de Chile and make our way to Caracas as best we could. I think this way we'd see more and be freer, and we'd be rid of the romantic air of continent-crossing bikers that surrounds us and distorts our view of reality.

The truck took us as far as Melleco. There we made another attempt to continue by bike, but as "Poderosa" was making ever louder and stranger noises, we decided to stop and ask for help from truck drivers, that long-suffering guild, who have helped us more than anyone.

While we waited, Fúser made maté and, as ever, the familiar taste combined with the beauty of the landscape inspired me to review everything we'd seen so far in Chile—the beauty of the Andes, the small farms golden with wheat, the rich orchards dripping with apples and pears. And in contrast, the downtrodden huasos, poorly dressed in their unfailing ponchos and frayed, wide-brimmed hats, on small horses as famished as the riders themselves, who turn to drink in an attempt to escape their poverty. I also thought of the typical foreman, who fills in for his absentee master and is repellent even in the way he dresses—like an off-duty matador, in a pinched, short black jacket, trousers tight down to the ankles, a tilted hard-brimmed hat and short boots adorned with huge spurs. This is the man who speaks ill of his farm hands, calling them drunkards and slackers, and does nothing to improve their lot. Instead, he thinks he's doing himself a favor by singing the boss's praises, without realizing that he's betraying himself and his class.

Suddenly a truck turned up and interrupted my ruminations. We hoisted up the poor old bike and went back to Los Ángeles. After a bit of negotiating, we found ourselves at the police headquarters talking to a couple of sergeants who'd been stationed on the Argentine border, where they had been fêted and wanted to repay the attention by inviting us home. On our way, they kept up their panegyrics in praise of Argentine hospitality, and as the way was long and the story short they repeated it over and over—each time enriching it and becoming more and more moved by their own tale.

Unfortunately the lady of the house did not feel the same enthusiasm for Argentines as her husband, and that night we went to bed with sorrow in our hearts and nothing in our bellies.

Los Ángeles, 28 February 1952

Last night we had one of the wildest and most interesting adventures of our trip. During the day we made friends with two girls who seemed interested in getting to know us. Soon we were on good terms and they introduced us to the head of the town's volunteer fire brigade. With the girls' support we persuaded him to let us spend the night where they keep the fire engines.

After dinner we went out with the girls. Once again we found a marked difference between the attitudes of women in Chile and in Argentina with regard to the opposite sex. Perhaps the fact that we are "birds of passage" makes things more possible, but I think the difference lies in their upbringing.

We ambled back to the fire station in silence, chewing over our respective experiences. The place where we were to sleep was narrow, with a slit for a window, and Fúser lay down beside it. He was in a state of agitation, but whether because of his asthma or the girl, I don't know. I tossed and turned in my sleeping bag, and when I got up for the umpteenth time I found a tiny stairway that led up to the roof. Climbing, I found myself in a kind of cupola, open on all four sides. It was cold, but I curled up in my sleeping bag and fell asleep.

I don't know how much time went by, but I was woken by a noise so deafening I felt my eardrums splitting. Leaping up, I felt a rope brushing my shoulder. It was the pull attached to the clapper of the fire bell. I had lain down to sleep right under the bell, just a couple of feet below it. The din and the vibrations were atrocious.

I hurled myself down the stairs to find Pelao already talking with the night watchman and asking him to let us help. The fire chief arrived and lent us a couple of helmets and protective jackets. Moments later we were racing along, clinging to the side of a fire engine called Chile-España.

After a mile or so we began to make out the glow of the flames, and then the typical smell of burnt resin you always get with conifers. In spite of the way we all pitched in, the building, which was made of pine timber and reeds, was almost completely destroyed. One group went at the brush fire that extended into the woods, while the rest of us attacked the house and an outbuilding.

I worked on one of the hoses, and Fúser removed the debris. When the blaze was under control, we heard the meowing of a cat trapped in the smoking remains of the roof. Fúser went to look for it in spite of the protests of the other firemen, who wanted to get back to their beds. But when Fúser came back with the kitten in his hands everyone applauded, and they decided to keep it as the station mascot.

On our way back we remarked on the chances that on our first night in Los Ángeles we should witness and help to fight a fire, but the explanation was simple enough. In this wooded area, there are almost 400 fires a year—some caused by accident, some by carelessness, and some by landowners who burn the woods to grow crops. So there are fires almost every day and sometimes two or three. The next day we were given pennants as souvenirs of our participation.

Santiago de Chile, 1 March 1952

In Los Ángeles we made contact with a truck driver who was moving furniture to Santiago. He charged us 400 Chilean pesos to carry our bike and took us on as porters for 50 pesos plus meals.

We bade farewell to our friends at the fire station, had a somewhat more affectionate send-off from the girls and set out for Santiago.

We reached the capital on Saturday. My first impression was that I was back in Córdoba, though the mountains here are higher and closer. We arrived at our destination and started unloading the truck. While we were working, Ernesto surprised me yet again with one of his extraordinary sallies.

As a joke we began to praise the strength of the truck driver's mate, who, to show off how tough he was, began unloading the heaviest pieces. The owner was watching us, and he started making sarcastic remarks about Argentines, saying we were all weedy and slackers. Fúser and I gave as good as we got. Little by little the truck driver lost his temper, and when he ran out of clichés to counter our banter he came on as the big boss. "Right, you two can carry that wardrobe," he told us. "That's what I hired you for."

The wardrobe in question was a vast piece of furniture made of extremely heavy wood, and it barely fitted through the narrow hallway. Ernesto and I were trying to maneuver it into position, but without much success. The driver's mate came to give us a hand, but his boss stopped him, saying, "Hold it right there, José. Let the lads from Buenos Aires manage on their own."

Pelao turned, looked the boss in the eye and said, "Look what I can do if I've a mind to." And turning to me, he added, "Mial, you stay out of this." Putting his arms round the wardrobe, he lifted it about four inches off the ground, carried it along the hallway and left it in the middle of the bedroom. Then he came back to where the three of us stood, dumbstruck by his performance, and announced, "That's me done." And he sat down on the curb beside the bike. I don't know where he found the strength to do what he did.

When we finished the job we took the bike to the workshop of an Argentine who lives in Chile. Then we went to the Argentine embassy to look for mail. There we met the consul, another candidate for our collection of shameless characters. He wanted us to believe he suffered from an occupational disease owing to the quantity of drink he had been obliged to consume at official functions. This had given him a gastric ulcer that he claimed would send him to the grave. Since he drinks like a fish, I think he'll be carried off by delirium tremens.

Farewell to "Poderosa II"—from bikers to stowaways

Santiago de Chile, 2 March 1952

Yesterday was Sunday, so we went out to see the city. We still held to our first impression—that it's very like Córdoba—though certainly bigger and more modern. Like good tourists we went to the zoo and Museum of Fine Arts. I didn't care for most of the paintings, except for a few by Lira and Smith, but I did like the work of the sculptors. Although they imitate the French school, these include some fine pieces—particularly the work of Rebeca Mata, which has character.

That afternoon we discovered that one of the Córdoba water-polo teams happened to be in Santiago—the Suquía team, coached by Espejo Pérez, a friend of mine since the 1943 strike. We went to see him at the pool where the match was to be held, and there we also ran into another old acquaintance—"Negro" Llovet, who used to play soccer with me on the Juniors team and spend summers at Bajada de Piedra. He's the goalkeeper.

After leaving our friends for the time being, we set out on a long, fruitless search for spare parts. Finally, we decided to leave the bike behind.

We converted two of the saddlebags into knapsacks and left everything else on the bike. As we wrapped it in the tent to protect it from the dust and damp, I felt as though we were placing a shroud on the dead body of a loyal friend. Surreptitiously I gave the bike a gentle pat and walked away, sad and upset.

A little while later we watched the water-polo match, shouting and rooting wildly for the Suquía lads. That night we had a farewell celebration, toasting in turn the joyful occasion of our chance encounter and—though they were sorry to see us go—the success of our difficult, though enviable, journey. All our feelings of regret soon vanished, and once more our usual cheer held sway.

Valparaíso, 7 March 1952

On the 4th, after saying goodbye to the water-polo team and giving them some letters home, we headed for the road that runs from Santiago to Valparaíso.

For more than four hours we watched a long series of trucks appear, pass us by and disappear, until at long last one of the drivers responded to our signals, braked and picked us up.

To get to Valparaíso you have to negotiate two small mountain ranges. Crossing the first by day, we were able to appreciate the beauty of the deep green valleys with scattered small farms full of orchards, many in flower and others bearing a handsome crop.

Snaking through the hills, the road on the far side of the mountain comes out into more arid and less heavily populated terrain. The second ascent was by night, and in this part of the mountains the cold gripped us like a vice. We ferreted ourselves between the cases that the truck was carrying. All we could see from there was the glare of headlights of one vehicle after another. The traffic on this road was extremely heavy.

We arrived at about ten o'clock at night. We said goodbye to the truck driver, shouldered our knapsacks and started walking.

The city center lies far below where the highway ends,

which was in a neighborhood that must have been built over the top of old wooden shacks. We made our way to a parking lot for coaches and trucks, and there, where the attendant had his hut, was a shack selling fried fish and the inevitable Chilean wine. We went in, drawn by the aroma, and came upon a rather drunk Argentine. Our presence stirred his alcoholic longings for home, and he offered us a few drinks and some fish.

The next day we befriended the owner of the fish shack. What a great guy! He has two elderly women working as cooks. One's practically deaf and the other, who looks like a medieval witch, is on the very threshold of senile dementia. They help him and he helps them, because I don't think anyone else would dare give them jobs. At the same time, he has a good laugh and keeps them happy, playing on the deaf woman's misunderstandings and especially taunting Rosita, the older of the two, with double entendres about her supposed love affairs, which she answers with offended modesty.

He has offered us lunch and dinner for the whole time we're here trying to organize a trip to Easter Island. This could put our tour of South America behind schedule, but it's an opportunity not to be missed.

Yesterday we were hoping to get to see a Mr. Molina Lucco, the only person who can give us authorization to make the trip to Rapa Nui. We came back to the fish shack for lunch and dinner. The owner is a true representative of the Chilean people in particular and of ordinary people in general. There isn't a beggar, a stray dog or cat whose hunger he doesn't stay with a scrap of fish. He wants to go to Argentina—to earn money, he says—but doesn't realize he'll never get rich with that heart of gold of his, because individual wealth is nothing but the exploitation of man by man.

Valparaíso is one of the prettiest and most strategically

situated cities in all of Chile. It has a handsome backdrop of a wooded mountain range and landscapes of the greatest beauty. There are glaciers less than thirty miles away where people can practice winter sports all year round. To the west the city is lapped by the waters of a beautiful wide bay, which forms attractive beaches a few miles further north in Viña del Mar. What's more, it is built in a strangely original way—some of the neighborhoods are linked to the center by long, steep stairways and others by cable cars.

That night we looked round several of these neighborhoods, especially the port, with its narrow, dirty streets full of bars and brothels, drunken sailors and clinging women. We thought we were in the Casbah in Algiers.

Yesterday at one of the shipping agencies we met the captain of a cargo ship bound for Antofagasta. We persuaded him to let us stow away, and if the port authorities don't nab us, we're going to work our passage.

On board the San Antonio, 8 March 1952

Once again I've had one of those adventures that are only possible when you make your dreams come true. This could never have happened had I stayed home selling cough syrup. At seven last night, after bidding farewell to the owner of the fish shack and having an obligatory drink or two, we headed for the port. Our clothes, knapsacks and especially our garish sleeping bags caught the attention of passers-by, as well as that of the policeman on guard at the entrance to the docks. He asked us where we were going, and we answered firmly that we were crew members of the San Antonio.

He sent us to get our baggage inspected by customs, but we must look honest, because they let us through without a check. Once on the wharf, we hid our gear in a coal truck that was tipped up beside the rails.

From the breakwater we could see the frenzied activity on board. Five hundred tons of various goods had to be loaded—provisions, cement, wine, and so forth. We tried to get on deck under cover of all this furious traffic, but we kept running into the officer on watch who, according to what we learned from the crew, is the company spy and would never let us sail.

Night was drawing on, and the wharf was gradually emptying. I felt as if everybody was watching us. We went up and down the entire length of the wharf several times. When night fell we curled up in the shadow of the truck where we'd left our knapsacks.

The minutes passed at a maddening snail's pace. The policeman walked past us three or four times, and so did the stokers, who kept the cranes' boilers alight. They almost stepped on us as they shouldered the sacks of coal.

Midnight came, and still the officer hadn't moved. At one o'clock in the morning the new shift of stevedores came on, and Fúser took advantage of the confusion to get on board to locate the toilets, where we were thinking of hiding.

Meanwhile I went over to one of the crane operators, because there was a breeze blowing fit to freeze a penguin. I managed to get him to invite me up. When Pelao got back from his reconnaissance he too took up lodging beside the boiler. We dozed off and on until five in the morning. The sun came up, a new shift of stevedores came on, and there was the officer still at his post, as rock-solid and unmoving as the ship's mainmast.

The crew arrived at about nine, and a gangplank was set up for them. Then and there we joined the queue. Once aboard we shoved the knapsacks under a tarpaulin that covered one of the lifeboats and got ourselves into the toilet.

Our first impression was not particularly pleasant. The toilet was out of order and was brimming over with shit, but this was no time to be fussy, so we bolted the door shut.

We didn't dare even breathe. When someone knocked at the door, I called out to say the toilet was in use. They left.

The minutes dragged as slowly as sweethearts making their way home after the cinema, and we got more and more nervous. If we felt like this, knowing the captain wasn't going to say anything and that the worst that could happen was that they'd chuck us off the boat, imagine what state a refugee would be in, fleeing persecution, knowing that if found he could lose his life.

At about eleven the engines started, but our great displays of silent jubilation did not last long. The engines slowed down and eventually stopped. Meanwhile, several people knocked on the door, but luckily there was another toilet and they used that.

At last at about twelve o'clock we heard the shrill whistle announcing that the engines were about to be started again. Then we heard the screeching of the anchor-chain and finally felt the ship begin to move.

The yellowish smudge we could make out through the tiny porthole slipped slowly by, then speeded up and was replaced by the blue of the sky and bits of ships' hulls. We hugged each other, wild with joy, even though we were still afraid we might be discovered. I stuck my head out through the porthole to bid farewell to Valparaíso bay. There was a guard of honor in the form of a huge flock of seagulls, flying about our heads like white handkerchiefs waving us goodbye, together with a great crowd of pelicans wishing us a safe journey in harsh but affectionate tones.

After we'd been under way for about two hours—prompted by hunger and the stench of the toilet—we decided to present ourselves on deck. We passed the galley and went in, and a kitchen boy gave us something to eat: some bread and raw onions, and coffee.

The captain called us up to the bridge, where he engaged in a bit of play-acting. As we climbed up the gang-way he gave us an exaggerated wink of complicity and then put on a comical air of severity, demanding loudly, "What do you think you're doing here? Don't you know you're compromising this ship's officers?" And on and on it went for several minutes, as he read us the riot act with a stream of reprimands. Then he called the boatswain and instructed him, "These gentlemen are under your orders. I can hardly throw them overboard now that they're here, but see you keep them busy, and let them find themselves somewhere to bunk down."

We were set to work straight away, me in the kitchen and Fúser cleaning the toilets. Until a few moments ago I had a dish-rag in my hands, washing up plates and cutlery, and then the cook got me peeling onions. Just then the ship began to roll and my stomach began to heave, so I had to take the bucket out and carry on peeling onions on deck. Pelao had already finished his fragrant task, and he took advantage to snap a picture of me "crying my eyes out."

On board the San Antonio, 9 March 1952

Last night, after cleaning the kitchen till it shone (the steward and cook want to squeeze every last drop out of us), we went up on deck for air. Amid the fluorescence of the moonlight on the sea, I saw flying fish for the first time in my life. When they jump out of the water they look like the most beautiful silver rockets.

All the sailors were asleep by then, and we headed for the bridge, where we could see a light. There we found the captain, an officer and the wireless operator playing canas-ta. We made our presence known, and when they found out that we knew how to play they invited us to join them. We played, and Pelao—who's very good—won three consecutive hands. They were determined to beat us, but couldn't manage it.

At about two o'clock in the morning the captain felt hungry and sent for the cook to be woken up. When the man saw who he had to serve—two of his own subordinates—he was absolutely livid and insisted that, come what may, we were going to help him. It was impossible, though, for at that moment the three other players were digging their heels in, utterly determined to beat us, and would never have let us up from the card table.

It wasn't long before the cook came back with five steaming omelettes, several bottles of wine and a filthy temper. We ate the omelettes, drank the wine and began losing—I don't know whether because of our post-prandial state or because if one of them didn't win a hand we would still have been playing when the sun came up.

The San Antonio, *10 March 1952*
As might have been expected, after the tension of the previous day and the drinks we had last night, I slept like a log and, of course, didn't hear the cook or the steward when they called me. When I got to the kitchen I had to bite my tongue and take everything they felt like shouting at me. I consoled myself by contemplating the calm beauty of the sea, and for the first time in my life I saw a pair of sperm whales blowing, with their spouts rising many feet in the air. I never knew it was possible to see sperm whales, or any other whales, in these latitudes.

One side of the coin—the Yankee copper mines

Antofagasta, 11 March 1952

Today, at about two in the morning, we docked in Antofagasta. We helped moor the ship, then, when the inspection party arrived, we hid in the captain's cabin. That was the last place they would think of looking for a pair of stowaways.

Off we went to see the sites. To get back on to the docks we said we'd arrived by train and were picking up some freight that was aboard the ship.

Although the steward's a miserable sod and can't bear the sight of us (since everyone from the captain down to the cabin boy treats us with deference), we're staying on board while we see if we can sort out a trip to Chuquicamata. To leave Chile without seeing the nitrate fields and copper mines would be a real pity.

Baquedano, 12 March 1952

When we'd looked into the possibilities open to us, we took our leave of the crew, shouldered our knapsacks and set off for the highway out of Antofagasta. We spent several hours on the road to Chuquicamata—some forty miles from Antofagasta—eventually arriving by truck.

The desert began after we'd been driving only a few minutes. The road winds between tall and totally arid hills. Not so much as a blade of grass to be seen the whole way, just the monotonous reddish-gray of the desert. The strip of asphalt and the telegraph poles are all that reveal that man has set foot in this lonely wilderness. There are stretches where patches of nitrate and gypsum show through on the surface of the desert sandstone. Every mile or two some of the posts are painted white to let travelers know there's a water outlet there, as it's piped in from the Bolivian border to supply all the tiny villages scattered across the desert.

As we drove deeper into the Chilean high-desert plateau, we realized that this was no empty phrase. Not even cactus grows in these desolate stretches. Nothing— that word says it all. Only a completely blue sky, some- times a little blurred on the horizon owing to the glare, with a few clouds that look as if they've been put there to decorate the landscape. Altogether it makes a wonderful scene. We took two or three photos. But you'd need a hun- dred photos or a lot of footage of technicolor film to cap- ture the imposing beauty of this place.

Now it's ten o'clock at night. I'm writing in a "hotel" by the light of a carbide lamp. Once again I have the two sides of the coin before me. On the one hand the beauty described above, as well as the wealth of this area, and on the other the event I am about to relate.

As we wandered about the village looking for some shelter, we met a poor working-class couple. The husband had been arrested as an alleged Communist and had spent three months in jail. Now he's fighting to be allowed to work in one of the local mines, which is very difficult when he's been labeled a Communist.

A little while ago I walked through the whole village again—one long string of houses with zinc walls, built along a single street bordered by the nitrate hills. The great majority of the houses are liquor stores, where the workers from the mines and the railway turn up to "cure" their woes by drinking themselves silly.

I came to a corner where two walls met and paused to contemplate the picture that Fúser and this couple made. By the light of only a scrap of candle and the moon, which was just rising over the hills, Ernesto was preparing maté while husband and wife shivered with cold, because the temperature had abruptly dropped, and they had only their ragged clothing to cover them. With his limited mode of speech, but with admirable conviction and accuracy, the husband was telling of the injustices meted out to him and his fellow-workers, many of whom had been murdered in Guachipato or weighted down and sunk in the ocean.

Unaware she was observed, his wife watched him as he spoke, and she showed a kind of entranced admiration that touched a sentimental chord in me. I felt something warm inside that linked me fraternally to this woman, poor in money and in culture but rich in feeling, who had faced up to a long string of setbacks, persecution and disasters and was loyal to her companion even in misfortune.

I broke into the circle formed by the light of the candle and handed the couple my blanket, suggesting to Fúser that we take another turn as far as the railway station to stretch our legs and avoid their outpouring of thanks.

We walked along the street by the light of the moon as far as the spit-and-sawdust bar where I'm writing now.

Chuquicamata, 13 March 1952
(Chuquicamata police station, 1st precinct)

We are comfortably lodged at the police station. As always, it's all a question of *trouver l'homme*. We ran into a police superintendent and a lieutenant, a couple of great guys, who quickly ironed out our difficulties. But I return to the 12th, at eleven o'clock at night.

When we got back from the bar we found our unfortunate companions huddled together in a corner. We got into Fúser's sleeping bag and tried to sleep.

A mischievous little breeze began whispering in my ear. It was not long before it had changed from mischievous to unpleasant, and from unpleasant to downright wicked. Beside me, Pelao was fast asleep and snoring, while I lay frozen to the marrow, cursing him and envying his fantastic capacity to sleep anywhere and under any condition. Each hour seemed interminable. When I thought several had passed, I'd look at my watch to find that only twenty-odd minutes had gone by. It was a very bright night, with the moon shining like daylight, and only a nearby hill cast a cone of shadow on the walls behind which we were sheltering. For want of anything better to do, I passed the time watching how, as the moon went down, this cone of shadow took possession of the path, of the railway fence and lastly of the railtrucks that were in my sight. Meanwhile Ernesto went on sleeping peacefully, and our neighbors were moving and breathing hard, whether copulating or trying to keep each other warm, I don't know. When the cold reached its maximum intensity, dawn began to break. Utterly unable to sleep, my limbs completely stiff with the cold and my awkward position, I decided to get up and walk around to get warm. Shortly after, my three companions followed suit.

By mid-morning, after saying goodbye to the couple, we managed to find a truck to take us as far as Calama, fifty-odd miles from Baquedano.

This stretch ran through desert too, and at an altitude of more than 6,500 feet. We saw several mirages, veritable lakes that were but optical illusions. The road ran parallel to a series of hills, crossing them just before reaching Calama. Up ahead rose the stately volcano of San Pedro, with its snow-covered summit.

In Calama we took what they call a gondola, which is just a truck adapted for use as a bus, and we reached the sentry post at the entrance to the mine. Just when we thought we were going to be kept waiting and questioned over and over again, we found that the police superintendent was a decent fellow, and he even gave us a preliminary tour round all the sections of the mine in the police van, accompanied by an affable and talkative lieutenant. (This journey is teaching me to get rid of certain prejudices. A worthy man can turn up where you least expect to find one.)

That evening they invited us to have supper in the police station. As far as we were concerned, it was breakfast, lunch, tea and supper in one. They lent us a couple of camp beds right there in the station. After our trials of the previous days we fell asleep on the spot. It had been a long time since we'd been able to rest like that.

Chuquicamata, 14 March 1952
We got up early and went to see Mr. Mackeboy, the mine's Yankee administrator. His Most Exacting Majesty, as we dubbed him, kept us cooling our heels for a long time. In his Yankeefied Spanish he informed us that this was not a tourist center or a charitable institution, and he lumbered us with a guide to take us round the mine.

Of course the tour we had today only served to confirm the opinion we formed when we went round yesterday—that is, that the whole place is incalculably rich.

The countless pieces of machinery, the perfect synchronization and the way they get the maximum use out of every element certainly inspire admiration, but this is eclipsed by the indignation aroused when you think that all this wealth only goes to swell the coffers of Yankee capitalism, while its true owners, the Araucanian people, live in abject poverty.

The first place we visited was the gallery of what's called an open-pit mine. It consists of a number of terraces about fifty or sixty yards wide and two or three miles in length. Here they drill and place the dynamite, blow up bits of the hill, and then use universal shovels—a kind of bulldozer—to load up the dump cars hauled by an electric engine. From there the ore goes to the first crushing mill, where a dumper tips it out.

After the first crushing, automatic conveyors take the ore to a second mill and then a third. When the rock is finely crushed it is treated with sulphuric acid in large tanks. All this solution of sulphates is taken to a building, which houses the vats of electrolyte for separating out the copper and regenerating the acid.

The copper obtained by electrolysis is smelted in large furnaces at a temperature of 2,000 degrees centigrade, and then this torrent of liquid copper is tipped into large molds dusted with calcined bone. It goes on into a unit that solidifies and cools it down almost instantaneously, and then electric cranes carry the molds to a mill, which planes them to a uniform thickness.

All this is done with such precision that it reminded me of the Chaplin film *Modern Times*. The impression grew even stronger when we tried to familiarize ourselves with various aspects of the technological process. Each worker or machine operator knows only what goes on in his section, and sometimes only part of it. There are many who have been working here for more than ten years and don't know what goes on or what gets done in the next section down the line. Of course this is encouraged by the company, which can more easily exploit them this way, as well as keep them at a very low level culturally and politically. The striving trade-union leaders have a titanic struggle to make the workers see the pros and cons of the agreements that the company tries to get them to sign. The company also employs other subtle means to combat the union.

The man acting as our guide, who is nothing but a filthy mercenary, told us that whenever there's an important union meeting, he and some of the administrator's other assistants invite a large number of miners to a brothel, thereby robbing the meeting of a required quorum. To give some idea of this character's mentality, it's enough to say that at one moment he was telling us that the workers' demands were excessive, and a little later he informed us that if the mine stood idle a single day the company lost a million dollars. With amounts like that at stake, this born slave dares to say that 100 pesos—a dollar—is an excessive demand. How we itched to throw him into one of the acid vats!

Chuquicamata, 15 March 1952

Today we went to see a new plant—without an official guide. It's being built to work the copper sulphides that are yet to be touched, which give a 30 percent yield. Some monumental furnaces are being built. One of the chimneys is more than 300 feet high—the tallest in South America. It is almost finished, and it was only to be expected that Fúser wasn't going to leave without going up to the top. We rode in a lift that takes the bricklayers. From the top you can look down over the whole extent of the mine and see how much wealth still remains to be extracted by the Braden Company.

When we came down we met one of the members of the union. He explained to us that the company pays low daily wages, but attracts workers by holding out the illusion that the company store sells goods at lower prices than those of other establishments in the area. But it turns out that there is only a limited number of cheap articles, and essential foodstuffs are not always in stock, so the men have to buy them at fabulously high prices elsewhere from establishments that operate hand-in-glove with the company. Of course, once a worker has settled here he stays on, hoping his demands will be heard and his needs met in the next contract. Time goes by, there's a wife, then children, and in the end, against his will and knowing he's being exploited, he remains until his eldest son takes his place, once he's been rendered useless by the passing years and privations—assuming he's not been killed in a blasting accident, or by silicosis or by the sulphuric vapors.

Afterward, we went over the western part of the town, where a plant makes prefabricated houses. This kind of building could solve the housing problems not only of Chuquicamata but also of the rest of Chile, if the technique were correctly applied, with a proper finish, nicely painted, and so on. Here everything is done on the cheap, just to give the workers housing that fulfills the minimum requirements—and sometimes not even that. Besides, they group the houses together in a distant part of town and don't provide any drains. Of course the Yankees and their lackeys have a special school for their children, as well as golf courses, and their houses aren't prefabricated.

We also visited the area scheduled to be mined over the next ten years, when the sulphide processing plant is finished. When we saw that they would get millions upon millions of dollars a day out of this area too (they are currently extracting 90,000 tons of ore a day), Fúser and I remembered that when we had read a book on Chile's copper we thought the author was exaggerating when he said that forty days' work could pay off all the capital investment. Life is certainly a great teacher and shows you more than a hundred books.

In the afternoon, following our tour, we have decided to continue our journey and head for another of the places that we've wanted to see ever since we read accounts of nitrate extraction in Chile—the lands where Lafertté[1] fought. When the moment came to say goodbye to the police, the lieutenant—who always agreed silently whenever we made some direct or indirect criticism of our guide—gave us a lift in his van as far as the road to Tocopilla, embraced us warmly and wished us a good journey.

En route to Iquique, 16 March 1952

After we said goodbye to the lieutenant yesterday we waited for a lift at the edge of the road, which runs beside a hill. The landscape is still an endless desert. The high plateau stretches away before us, completely flat, with the sun and clouds making it look like an enormous white carpet dotted with black specks. The scene lies within an amphitheater formed by the hills, and although the wind was quite strong where we were, we could see a diesel tractor with its smokestack, looking like a toy from our vantage point, emitting puffs of smoke that remained motionless out on the plain.

As we contemplated the landscape and discussed how much we had learned in only forty-eight hours, night drew on without any vehicle giving us a lift. So as not to have to go back to the police station, which was several miles away, we went to the sentry posts at the entrance. After getting permission we settled down in our sleeping bags, feeling famished, because the corporal on duty was the only one of the cops who didn't take to us, so that although there were leftovers from the mess, he didn't offer us any.

When the light woke me up at dawn I noticed that where he slept Pelao was almost touching the corporal's

---

[1] Elías Lafertté (1886–1961), Communist trade unionist who led the struggle for the rights of workers in the nitrate mines of Chile prior to the Second World War.

boot as he sat dozing on a bench. The scene left me with an unpleasant feeling, but I didn't mention it to Fúser for fear he would pull my leg about it. It still sticks in my mind, though.

Today is a magnificent day. I could gaze at this landscape for ever. The hills look like enormous hunchbacks furrowed with wrinkles. The sky is the deepest blue with tiny clouds that bring out the beauty of its color even more.

It's three in the afternoon. We've set ourselves up in a tent made out of Fúser's blanket. This morning we set off in a truck that took us out as far as the north–south highway. We got to the crossroads at about twelve o'clock, and the truck driver left us there, telling us that there was a clump of trees about ten miles away—the only one for hundreds of miles around—where we could rest until the sun was less intense. In spite of the fierce sun and the fact that it was the wrong time of day for walking, we set out. We covered the first stretch easily, but the oppressive heat and the weight of our knapsacks gradually sapped our strength, and as the clump of trees gave no sign of turning up we decided to make camp. We put our tent up, taking advantage of a telegraph pole—the only sign of civilization in this immense desert—and here we wait either for a charitable truck driver to turn up or for the wrath of the sun to abate somewhat so that we can go on in pursuit of this famous clump of trees.

As a point of interest I should like to place on record that this region has the lowest rainfall in the world, without a millimeter of water falling for several years together.

But what beautiful desolation! How I wish I could describe it or capture it on canvas! The heat is so intense and the light so brilliant it creates shimmering reflections that form a kind of patina, blurring and softening the hills on the horizon, where they are forever crowned with motionless clouds that never spill a drop of water on the high plateau, but only in the valley or valleys on the far side of the hills. These reflections and the shadows cast by the clouds combine to produce an optical phenomenon. It looks as if the sands are rising and falling like the waves of the sea.

In the land where Lafertté fought

I'm sitting in one of the main squares of this charming city. While enjoying the shade of the trees here I am going to bring my diary up to date and relate the events of the few days that have gone by since the 16th.

At about five o'clock a car came by and gave us a lift. Its three occupants were completely drunk. The road we covered was short but quite picturesque. The car described a series of S-bends, while the driver sang cuecas as tunelessly as humanly possible. From time to time he let go of the steering wheel and beat time on the bodywork with both hands. There can be no doubt but that the god Bacchus was watching over us, for in spite of everything the vehicle managed to stay on the road. At last we reached a railway station, where our ways parted. We got out heaving a sigh of relief. By then our hosts had moved on from the euphoric stage of their binge, and dense storm-clouds were gathering over their hitherto peaceful, alcoholic heavens.

We prepared to spend the night there and made our way toward the station house to ask for hot water to brew maté. It wasn't long before all the bored inhabitants of the railway station were drawn by the presence of a couple of strangers, and they began circling us like birds of prey round a carcass, until the most impatient or the boldest ventured a question, and we answered it. One exchange led to another, and it wasn't long before we had struck up that easy camaraderie that is always established between young people when both parties seek it.

As it had grown very dark, one of the lads brought a kerosene lamp and another a guitar, and what with the music and songs and tales of our journey, soon we were all old mates. Someone invited us to share their dinner and we went on chatting until after midnight. We were offered a bedroom, a zinc shed, which the rats seemed to find quite cozy. Dozens of them went scurrying away between the camp beds, perhaps annoyed by our intrusion.

While I was trying to get to sleep I thought back on the sculptural ensemble presented by the group of lads as they sat gathered round the guitarist. In the weak light of the oil lamp they gave the impression of figures carved from stone. With their high cheekbones, they looked like statues reflecting their Quechua heritage. I lay there thinking that all these good and generous people who have helped us all the way through Chile are the amalgam of Indians and poor Spaniards. Although the latter brought with them the vices and gold-fever of their leaders, they also brought the nobility and will power of the Hispanic race. Finally I fell asleep.

We arrived at the Empresa Salitrera de Toco the next afternoon. A group of road-builders was playing soccer, and they immediately invited us to join in, so we did. After the game we all went off together to eat dinner and sleep, with such open-handed familiarity that we could have been old friends.

We slept in the road-builders' camp, which consisted of two rooms made out of zinc sheets. There were more than eight of us in each room. The beds are bits of wood laid on top of tree-stump supports, but all the discomfort and overcrowding paled into insignificance beside the friendliness and warmth of the inhabitants.

We went to bed early, because they work from two until ten in the morning so as to avoid the merciless afternoon sun. Before going to sleep we took part in an original, stinking and extremely loud farting contest, in which despite our reputation we found ourselves ignominiously relegated to last place.

The next day we went to see two nitrate works—Rica Aventura and Prosperidad. They use the Shank extraction method, an old method that consists of separating the different components of the caliche (soil with a high saltpeter content) by means of hot water, thanks to the fact that the different salts have different levels of solubility at particular temperatures. This allows them to separate out first the sodium nitrate, then the potassium nitrate, then the perchlorates and finally the iodine.

As soon as we set foot on the first of the nitrate fields we realized that this was a foreign company, not just because of the tenacious exploitation of the resources, which would enable them to pay off new investments in a year, but because all the staff and most of the workers to whom we spoke seemed to have their brains colonized. They don't want to know they're being dispossessed, that they're being paid the lowest possible wages, and that they're kept in the depths of ignorance by the very same people who are getting rich from their labor and from Chile's nitrate fields.

After seeing and asking as much as we could, we went back to the road-builders' camp, where there was something different in the air—comradeship, I suppose—that sets it apart from the workers in the nitrate fields.

There was a truck-load of timber heading north the next day, so we said goodbye to the lads and moved on. We waited for another lift in a hamlet called Laguna, where the heat was unbearable. The whole of the little village sweltered in the burning sun. A dozen threadbare, weary-looking individuals watched us with scant curiosity as we arranged our knapsacks in the shade of a corridor by the bar and the pool hall and settled down to wait until we could continue our journey.

At dawn today, just as we were washing our faces in a nearby water tank, a truck loaded with alfalfa got a puncture. We hastened to offer our services and the driver paid us back by giving us a lift.

As I lay watching the sun come up over the sandy hills this morning, wrapped up in my sleeping bag and half buried in the sweet-smelling grass, I thought to myself that this was what I had always wanted—a journey like this, with no other concern than to see and get to know our America by my own means.

Fúser lay beside me reciting lines from Neruda[1] under his breath. I think he knows all the poems in the *Third Residence on Earth* and the *Twenty Love Poems and a Song of Despair* by heart. I caught the bug myself and chimed in for a minute with the only lines I know:

> I have written about time and water,
> described mourning and its purple hues;
> I have written about the sky and the apple,
> now I write about Stalingrad.

Our poetic euphoria was interrupted by the spectacle that now presented itself before us—the sea. We were on the crest of the mountain, and from where we sat on a cushion of alfalfa in the back of the truck we could see the whole road winding and unwinding like an enormous snake that crushed the mountain in its coils, and at the end of the road lay the blue mirror of the picturesque bay of Iquique, where we now are.

[1] Pablo Neruda (1904–73), Chilean poet and diplomat. His *Canto General* (1950) is an epic history of the Americas. He was awarded the Nobel Prize for Literature in 1971.

Arica, 22 March 1952

We slept in Iquique and then managed to get another truck to give us a lift to Arica. The road runs through desert here too, and to get to the city you have to cross what people around here call the Seven Pampas. These are seven high desert plains separated from one another by jagged sierras. The road runs for mile after mile across a vast desert plain, and then a corniche road crosses the mountain range, which rises to about 6,500 feet. This road is extremely steep and narrow, and it climbs up and down the mountain in the space of a few miles. The sierras form immense canyons very similar to those of Cuesta de Miranda, in the Andes of La Rioja, in Argentina, but instead of deep red, the rock here is reddish-gray. In some places the road runs so high that the clouds and the condors were floating beneath our feet.

Here and there were plaques commemorating the advance of the conquistadores Almagro[2] and Valdivia[3] and their troops, who marched from Peru to the south of Chile. When I think how difficult it is to make this journey now, by truck and over a road built for the purpose, I have to admire the courage, stoicism and tenacity of those Spaniards who undertook such a terrible journey, weighed down by their cuirasses and suits of armor, and reached their goal. What a pity that the courage they brought to the conquest of a hostile landscape was later turned to cruelty against its inhabitants!

On the way we saw two or three valleys that have water, and there we found tropical agriculture and vegetation very different from what we are used to. There were guava trees, mangoes, avocados and particularly the curious papaya plant, which looked to our South American

[2] Diego de Almagro (1475–1538), Spanish conquistador who joined forces with Francisco Pizarro in the conquest of Peru.
[3] Pedro de Valdivia (1500–54), Spanish conquistador who took part in the conquest of Venezuela, Peru and Chile.

eyes like a little palm tree with its trunk clustered with melons.

Only the maize sown in the fields makes us think we are in northern America near the equator. In fact, we're very near the Tropic of Capricorn.

After driving for almost twenty-four hours we reached Arica. We had a look round the port, went to the regional hospital in the afternoon and introduced ourselves to the director, who received us with deference. He is interested in laboratory work. We agreed to give him a theoretical and practical demonstration of the Ziehl-Nielsen colorimetric test using Twin 80 instead of heat.

Last night we slept at the hospital. Today we did the practical, as agreed, and ended up talking more about our journey than about science. This afternoon we went to the beach and stayed in the sea until the sun went down. Fúser hadn't had a bout of asthma since we left Valparaíso, but he felt a bit unwell after swimming for so long.

I'm really enchanted with the port. As we wandered about there, we came across a series of shellfish completely unknown on the Atlantic coast, and not only did we see them but we tasted them too. The one I liked best is a kind they call locos, and an enormous crab. Both are delicious and nutritious.

En route to Tacna, 23 March 1952
We went to the customs post at Chacalluta, which lies on the southern bank of the River Lluta and is Chile's northernmost point.

It seems as if it were only yesterday, but today marks thirty-eight days since we first set foot on Chilean soil at Casa Pangue, more than 2,000 miles to the south. We've seen the beautiful southern lakes with their cold climate and continuous rain, passed through the fertile central region full of beautiful cities and been to one of the biggest, richest and driest deserts in the world.

But more than anything we've found and confirmed that all the best and most generous of Chile is in its ordinary people, that we hadn't been wrong in choosing the poor over the rich and the revolutionary over the reactionary or the conformist.

As we were talking about all this, Fúser surprised me as usual by reciting some lines of poetry about the poor of the earth and the rivers in the mountains.

"Neruda?" I asked.

"No," he answered, "Martí."[4]

---

[4] José Martí (1853–95), Cuban poet, writer, political thinker and activist, hero of several of his country's attempts at independence from Spain and the USA. He died in battle in Dos Ríos, eastern Cuba.

In the land of the Incas

Tacna, 24 March 1952

Once we had finished with the consular and customs formalities we went out to see the city. It is extremely picturesque and noticeably different from Arica, only a few miles to the south. There is a very marked Quechua or Aymara influence to be seen in many aspects of everyday life here. Heading toward the outskirts, the central streets turn into alleyways that snake between little market gardens. As a remembrance of the Inca system there is no such thing as a wire fence. Only a line of reeds, pomegranate or fig trees mark the boundaries between the different properties.

On our way we met various Indian women riding donkeys and wearing the traditional clothing that we've seen only in pictures or at folk festivals—wide skirts, ponchos and their traditional bowler hats. They were taking their produce—watermelons, pumpkins, bananas, chili peppers, ocumos[1] and so on—to market.

We stuffed ourselves on figs and grapes, but were disappointed when it came to pomegranates, as they seem to be the local birds' favorite treat. They devour all the fruit through a tiny, almost imperceptible hole, leaving the outside apparently intact.

Sicuani, 30 March 1952
We're waiting at the police post of the Peruvian Civil

[1] Ocumo: a plant with yellow flowers and an edible root.

Guard to see if we can get someone to give us a lift to Cuzco. I'm feeling happy but nervous, because I'm itching to get there and see the life of the exploited Quechua Indians at first hand, to really feel the wonders of the Inca civilization. To see for myself, not through the prose of Inca Garcilaso[2] or the novels of Ciro Alegría, what remains of the Inca kingdom and its splendors, destroyed by the avarice of Pizarro and the Spanish Empire and exploited today by Peruvian landowners. To try and calm down I came and sat with my diary to record what has happened so far.

On the 24th, just as we were about to take out the crumpled soles that I guard jealously along with my pistol, a young Indian came up to tell us that a sergeant we had met was in pain and wanted us to examine him. We tended him, gave him an injection of papaverine and a bit of psychotherapy, and he soon felt better. Shortly afterward, another sergeant arrived to take over his post. He invited us to stay, to eat and sleep there until he could send us to Cuzco. He turned out to be an extraordinary character. He started talking about the beauties of Peru and its Inca ruins, which filled us with enthusiasm. But he spoke in such affected phrases, peppered with obscure terms that had nothing to do with what he was talking about, that it was difficult to follow his story. Sometimes he couldn't find the right word, and then he would stop stock-still until it came to him, and off he would go again, firing his elaborate Gongoristic phrases at us. Fúser and I stood it as long as we could, dying with laughter, and in the end we went off to get some sleep.

On the 25th we whiled away a few pleasant hours in the company of two sisters, the daughters of a Japanese family, whom we met this morning (and from whom we

[2] Inca Garcilaso (c.1540–c.1616), Spanish writer born at Cuzco, the son of an Inca princess and a conquistador. Wrote *Comentarios,* a moving description of the legends and beliefs of his mother's peoples.

scrounged lunch), while we waited to get a driver who was a friend of theirs to take us as far as Tarata, a major stop on the way to Lake Titicaca.

At first the road reminded us of northern Chile, but as we climbed higher the mountains went from sandy to rocky and took on that coppery color characteristic of the Andes we know. The hillsides were empty desert to begin with, but first a few cactus began to appear, then espinillos and pepper trees and later some yellow-flowering shrubs, and in the end all the hillsides were green. This color in the landscape filled me with incredible happiness and euphoria.

Soon we arrived in a little town called Estaque. If the genuine Aymara civilization still exists anywhere it's here, both in the architecture and in the dress and customs of the inhabitants.

The real climb began as we left the town. The mountains rose higher, and instead of a gentle slope the incline becomes a sheer abyss at the bottom of which a foaming torrent goes cascading down.

Great waterfalls that cut the road every few miles came into view, and at last we saw the first cultivated mountainsides. These are almost perpendicular slopes, but thanks to the system of terraces the Aymara grow potatoes, maize, chili peppers, and so on. The terraces are little horizontal platforms in which the earth is retained by means of a kind of border made of stones arranged one on top of another. It is both really interesting and lovely to see all these terraces, each a different shade of green, cut in symmetrical steps and with a special added touch of color by the Indian women in their bright clothing.

The maize they grow here must be genetically identical to the crop grown in America since before the Discovery. It is distinguished by the dark purple husk that protects the fruit, and the white cob with splashes of purple.

Next we came to a traditional indigenous village, with its low houses and truncated streets, some of which can be as much as a hundred feet higher than those running parallel to them. At the entrance to the village there are some canals running above the level of the road, and where the road cuts across the canal they've made pipes of hollowed tree trunks that go over the road like a bridge.

Of all the men traveling in the truck we were the only ones of European descent; all the others were pure Aymara. Looking at them I couldn't help thinking of the gauchos in Molina Campos's paintings—coppery complexions, broad flat noses, prominent cheekbones, some with sparse mustaches, wide mouths and small eyes like certain Asians. All were poorly dressed and either barefoot or wearing thong sandals. All of them without exception chewed coca uninterruptedly throughout the trip.

Although people say they are retiring and hostile, they talked and laughed with us all the time. Of course, a lot of them didn't speak Spanish, but those who did needed no coaxing to tell us about anything we asked them.

We reached Tarata, which in Aymara means fork in the road, at about five o'clock in the afternoon. For a few moments we stood contemplating a wonderful contrast. While the little town shone in the sun that burned over our heads, a few miles away beyond the fork we could see snow falling. An uncommon sight!

While we were looking for somewhere to spend the night we came upon a group of recruits playing basketball. We went over and, although the village lies at a height of more than 8,000 feet and—according to the experts—we shouldn't have been able to move, we joined in and didn't feel any lack of air at all. Pelao didn't even remember that he suffers from asthma.

The truck-bus left for Ilave at three o'clock in the morning. The engine roared into life and the vehicle began to climb. The cold was unbearable. The first couple of hours were boring, but at about five o'clock in the morning the sun came up and the peaks of the Andean foothills appeared, covered in snow. The vegetation disappeared again.

The mountain is covered with a kind of moss that acquires a woody consistency and is used as fuel by the herders looking after llamas and vicuñas.[3] We soon reached the highest point, called Ilave, 16,000 feet above sea level. There was already snow lying across the road. The crystals of ice sparkled like an infinite number of tiny diamonds. The whole of the landscape went from the pale blue of the snow through the slightly darker blue of the clouds formed by the heat of the sun and the light blue of the hills, culminating in the deep blue of the sky. The combination and range of color is stunning.

By the time we crossed the last of the snowy hills the clouds formed by the snow's evaporation were already enormous. Their blue contrasted with the coppery red of the hills without snow on them, and these in turn were splashed with the green of the moss. It was a very different spectacle from the previous scene, but no less beautiful.

At the highest point of the road we saw a mound, formed by thousands of small stones piled up, with a wooden cross on top. Most of the passengers spat outside as we passed, and one of them crossed himself. I leaned over to the most educated of them and asked him what this meant. He told me that the mound was an Apacheta, and that each traveler who walks by leaves a stone there, and with it he leaves behind his sorrows, ailments and bitterness. Being aboard the truck, they spat instead and with the spittle they got rid of all the evil they carried with them.

---

[3] Vicuña: a tawny-colored cud-chewing Andean mammal similar to the llama.

"And what about the cross?" I asked him.

"The priest put it there to confuse the Indians," he said.

He explained to me how the priest makes an amalgam of religions out of the cross and the Apacheta, tries to confuse the Indians, and in the end passes them off as Catholics. That way he can say there are thousands of believers in his parish, when in fact they still believe in Paccha Mama[4] and Viracocha[5] under a different guise.

I went on thinking for a long time about the beauty and poetry of the Apacheta, the criminal behavior of the priest, and about this Indian—poorly clothed and fed even worse—who had been able to explain this historical and social phenomenon in so few words, with a clarity and depth that a well-dressed and very well-paid professor would have envied.

This is one side of the coin, I told myself, the beauty of the landscape and a man capable of standing up for himself. But here's the other side: the rest of the Indians sharing this journey with us, a shapeless mass of drowsy beings, a race who for five centuries have been taught to think they are inferior, defeated and fit only for slavery, while at the same time they have been numbed by coca and alcohol.

They are so used to being ill-treated and humiliated that when we got into the truck, unable to see anything because it was so dark, we accidentally stepped on several people who were curled up on the floor, but not one of whom so much as uttered a word of complaint or warning.

By this time we were already on the high plateau, which is quite similar to the area preceding Patagonia— that is to say, mountains that form veritable Roman amphitheaters surrounding plains covered in tall wild

---

[4] Paccha Mama: mythical goddess of the Incas who represented Mother Earth.
[5] Viracocha: mythical god of the Incas, "the creator of man and the rest of the divinities."

grasses, where flocks of llamas, alpacas and vicuñas come down to graze. This area—full of animals and watered by the river Huenque, alive with trout—made me imagine what it might be like to make this same trip in a caravan with my brothers, seeing everything, fishing and hunting. It would be wonderful.

On the 26th we began to follow the shores of Lake Titicaca. We reached Puno at about six o'clock in the evening and immediately rushed down to the lake as if afraid it was about to disappear.

It looked very small to us at first, but what we were looking at was actually a small inlet or bay of the lake that lay between the peninsulas of Capachica and Chucuíto. We climbed the Chucuíto promontory and there before us spread the famous lake, vast, silent and serene. For Pelao and me it was one of the milestones of our journey. (The next is nearby too—Machu Picchu.) I felt so happy, as did Pelao. We shook hands in silence, and then Ernesto said, as if in answer to a question, "True to our principles and decisiveness, it's all turned out so well."

I didn't answer, because it had all been said, but I plan to remain principled and decisive.

On the 27th we went back to the lake to see if we could get out on the water. This proved impossible, because we couldn't make ourselves understood by any of the few fishermen we met. That afternoon we went to the UNICEF dispensary, which was running a fumigation campaign to eradicate malaria. Chatting with the doctor in charge, I discovered that there was a leprologist working in Cuzco—a Dr. Hermosa, whom I'd met in 1950 at a skin and syphilis conference in Tucumán, in Argentina. So I'll present myself there and we'll see what sort of reception we get.

At six in the morning on the 28th we embarked in a

truck making the Puno–Juliaca run. It was packed. But just as we left town, thanks to the inimitable art of truck drivers—who are true pioneers in the science of using inter-atomic spaces—we managed to squeeze in about twenty cases of potatoes, five barrels and four or five more passengers.

The landscape in this area is more arid than around the lake, and since it slopes down toward the sea it only ever rains here in summer; in winter it freezes, but never snows.

The journey was rough, passing through small towns with houses made of adobe and streets so narrow the truck can hardly get through them.

When we got to Juliaca we called in at the police station as usual. Then we went out to get some lunch (which cost three soles) and when we got back we found there was no chance of traveling any farther that day.

Not long after that a sergeant rolled into the police station as drunk as a skunk, bringing with him an officer, equally saturated with ethyl alcohol. After swearing and cursing at his subordinates he started in on us, but we won him round and it wasn't long before we were as thick as thieves. He invited us to have a drink. We accepted unanimously. We went out into the street to a bar a few paces away from the police station. The sergeant called for a bottle of pisco,[6] and just to show what a man he was he drew his revolver and aimed a shot overhead. The bullet ricocheted off one of the walls, then off the ceiling and hit a nearby table. Naturally enough we did not find this very amusing, and neither did the owner of the bar. It was not long before a captain in the Civil Guard turned up and held a brief discussion with the sergeant in private. The sergeant looked at me and asked with exaggerated signs of

---

[6] Pisco: Peruvian liquor made from fermented cane sugar.

complicity, "Che,[7] argentino, haven't you got any more firecrackers?"

Of course, I went to his aid and said no, I didn't have any more, and in fact it was me that threw the firecracker. Meanwhile I signaled to the captain as if to say: I'm only saying this to keep this drunkard, your subordinate, out of trouble.

Just then we heard a truck sounding its horn to announce it was about to set out, and we seized the opportunity to duck out.

We took the truck, which was heading for Cuzco. The load was more heterogeneous than on our previous trips. Of course, most of the passengers were Indians—almost all Quechuas rather than Aymaras—but there were half-castes too, as well as people from the coast, meaning people with a higher percentage of European blood.

We hadn't been going long when we got caught in the rain. A tarpaulin was quickly put up, because each and every one of the Europeanized and half-caste passengers started shouting and kicking up a fuss. On our way to Puno a few days before, on the other hand, when the only travelers were Indians and the two of us, there'd been a torrential downpour and only "their white majesties" Fúser and Mial got invited to move into the cab, despite the presence of Indian women both young and old, who were just as exposed to the rain as we were. In spite of our protests and resistance—we were ashamed to take precedence over the women—we ended up giving in and moving inside.

---

[7] "Che" is an expression generally used in Latin America to refer to people from Argentina as it is an interjection they often pepper their conversation with. It was his Cuban comrades in Mexico, while training for the invasion of the island, that nicknamed Ernesto "El Che." Nobody knows the origin of the word: it could be Guaraní or Mapuche (two Indian tribes of the continent) or it could have come from Andalucía with the conquistadores. In any case Guevara promptly adopted it and went as far as signing bank notes in Cuba simply "Che" when he was Governor of the National Bank.

The squall turned into a hailstorm, which fortunately didn't last long, because the tarpaulin was in no state to stand up to the impact of the hailstones for long.

Soon it was night. Along with a couple of guys from Arequipa we started up a few songs, and then the pisco went round to ward off the cold, and in the end I started chewing coca to see what it was like.

All through the long run new passengers kept getting on as others got off, most of them Indian women with their children. Watching them confirmed my first impression of how loving they are with their offspring. They treat them with greater tenderness than I have seen in other races. They play with them all the time and give them whatever they can to eat, day and night. The little ones seem to be insatiable.

The landscape here is like that of the north of Patagonia—that is to say, high and level plateaux surrounded by hills. There are a few flocks of alpaca to be seen again, but generally speaking there are more llamas and sheep. According to what I was told, the alpacas and the vicuñas have to live in very high places where the grass they eat is very tough, because if they graze on softer plants their teeth grow far too long, as can happen to beavers.

At dawn we had several more downpours. What bothered me most was the nausea I felt from my experiment with chewing coca.

We reached Sicuani. Like all the towns in the sierra it has a small central square flanked by the church and the municipal buildings. Next to the square is the market, where the Indian women sit by their steaming cooking pots in vociferous confusion, selling soups, chili stews, corn on the cob, boiled cassava and all kinds of other things to eat, many of which were unknown to us.

We had lunch and then went to ask for lodgings at the

police station. As at other times, they were suspicious of us at first, but the more they let us talk, the more we won their confidence, and they ended up offering us dinner and a place to sleep.

We went out to look round the town and met a guy who was really crazy. He said he was descended from the last chiefs of that region. He invited us to drink tea and listen to some of his compositions for the flute. He played us one, and it was so bad that even Pelao noticed it. We drank the tea and said a hasty goodbye. We went on looking round the town and making plans for a future journey by caravan.

We're still here at the Civil Guard post, expecting to leave for Cuzco at any moment.

Machu Picchu at last

Cuzco, 31 March 1952

We left Sicuani at about nine o'clock in the morning. The landscape here is more subtropical, and you can see little properties with their plots of different crops perfectly marked out. One curious thing in this area is that they grow everything at the same time. Right now they're reaping the wheat, harvesting the maize and gathering in the beans—all simultaneously.

The road runs along the right bank of the Vilcanota, which gets bigger and faster as an ever increasing number of brooks run into it. The sierras are covered with flowering broom. The road rises and falls according to the whim of the landscape. Sometimes it runs 500 yards above the roaring waters, and sometimes the passengers are splashed with a cold spray.

The truck-bus was full to the gunnels with a mosaic of Indians, half-castes and whites. Workers on their way to the plantations, students going to take exams at the university, servants, schoolchildren and so on. As usual we noticed that the half-castes are the ones who treat the pure Indians with the greatest cruelty.

Everyone pays the agreed price, but when a half-caste or a white gets in they think they have the right to turn any Indian out of their seat—be it a man or a woman carrying a child—and sit down comfortably themselves. The poor Quechuas, who have been inculcated for generations with the belief that they are inferior and fit only for slavery, and who know that any rebellion on their part will be harshly punished, give in and sit where they can.

For the rest, the journey was full of ups and downs—it was hot, then it rained, and later a hailstorm split the tarpaulin and we all got soaked. We took our revenge by stealing some corn on the cob from the woman who owned the truck, an exploitative half-caste who despises her own blood, and we left without paying the fare.

Here we are in the navel of the world, which is what the Indians call Cuzco. Now we're in the very heart of Quechua and Aymara America.

Today we began looking at the architecture straight away. The churches are a wonder. They clearly show the fusion of baroque and churrigueresque art with indigenous art. Unfortunately, in their ignorance and their irrational religious fanaticism the Spanish priests wanted to prove that their God was more powerful than Viracocha and they built their churches on top of the ancient Inca sun temples, thus destroying a great artistic and historical heritage.

This afternoon we went to the museum. I met an Indian girl in charge of the ceramics section who was quite something. She played hard to get, but I think she's more in need of it than I am and has been fasting just as long, and that's saying something.

We met at the National Library that night. I've been reading Manuel E. Cuadro's *History and Architecture of the Churches of Cuzco*, and I took notes so as to go round the churches again tomorrow with a greater appreciation of their styles. It seems that Viracocha took his revenge on the priests, because the 1950 earthquake toppled almost all the church towers.

Cuzco, 1 April 1952
I went back to the museum this morning with the double
aim of improving my cultural knowledge and working on
the Indian girl. I shall concern myself here with the first of
these.

The pottery is very similar to that made by the Diaguita
Indians in the north of Argentina, which is understandable
since that area was under Inca domination for several centuries. Both the pottery and the metalwork show finer
technique than anything I've seen before today.

There are specimens in the hall of anthropology that
show that the Quechuas successfully practiced the
trepanation of the skull, which means they had a level of
civilization similar to that of the Egyptians.

Among the most interesting exhibits is a series of figures and idols made out of a material called champis, an
alloy of copper, tin, silver and gold. Many of the figures
represent humorous pornographic scenes with a wit and
good taste that speaks volumes for the artistic talent of
their craftsmen.

We were shown a collection of emeralds depicting idols
and chiefs or kings, as well as gold figures of llamas and
vicuñas, but these are more valuable for the material
they're made of than for their beauty. But there are also
some vessels with handles resembling birds or pumas,
which are exceedingly beautiful. We found them similar
to Assyrian figures, which could confirm the theory that
there was a migratory flux from Asia to pre-Inca America.

We went to visit churches that afternoon, our notes at
the ready. The wealth of offerings contained in many of
them is incredible. The solid gold monstrance in the
cathedral (according to the little sign) weighs two arrobas,
or twenty-nine pounds seven ounces, and contains 2,200
precious stones.

While all this gold lies idle, María Magdalena, the

Indian girl, told me there are schools without books, for want of money to import them from Argentina.

At lunchtime we looked up Dr. Hermosa's address in the telephone book and that afternoon, as I was strolling with María Magdalena, I got her to take me as far as his surgery, which is some distance from the areas I'm familiar with.

I went into the waiting room. It was empty, and when the nurse came out I told her I wanted to see the doctor and to say that the request was from Dr. Granado. "Have you brought a letter from him?" the girl asked.

I had to explain that, despite my patched gaucho trousers and my rather grubby leather jacket, the Dr. Granado in possession of a university degree was none other than myself.

She showed me in. Hermosa didn't recognize me. Fortunately, there was a photograph on the wall taken during one of his study trips to Argentina. It showed mutual friends and leprosy specialists such as Olmos Castro, Argüello Pitt, Garzón and others. I went through their names as I reminded him that we had both been present at the 1950 skin and syphilis conference in Tucumán and recalled the night we had spent drinking gin together and listening to Atahualpa Yupanqui.[1]

He then recognized me and put himself at my disposal. I arranged to go back with Ernesto the next day—that is, tomorrow. Then I left because patients had started arriving.

The Indian girl was still waiting for me when I came out, rather surprised by my metamorphosis from globe-trotter to scientist. I should say that she, like 90 percent of the people we met in Cuzco, claims descent from one of the most ancient Quechua families.

---

[1] Atahualpa Yupanqui (1908–92), Argentina's foremost folk-music composer, guitarist and singer.

Cuzco, 2 April 1952

My interview with Dr. Hermosa was very fruitful. He offered to help us get to Machu Picchu, and he lent us his own Land-Rover to visit Ollantaytambo.

The road climbs too steeply at first and is not very pleasant, but it soon enters the Valley of the Incas, where everything changes. The whole mountainside is under cultivation, sometimes up to such great heights that the ploughmen and their oxen look like insects stuck up on a promontory.

The farther we went, the more we became aware of the grandeur of the mountain range that forms the other wall of the valley. The color of the rocks, the snow-covered summits shrouded in clouds, and the lush green of the slopes all made me wish fervently that the five of us Granados could be here to admire all these wonders together. Every now and then I imagined that the vehicle was ours and that all the family were making this journey. The whole place warrants sitting down with a palette of paints and not leaving until the picture is finished.

We reached the bottom of the valley. Our vehicle made its way along tracks bordered by flowering broom and shaded by capulíes and eucalyptus trees. The warm, crystal-clear air, the beautiful flowers and the roaring Vilcanota—everything about this journey makes it unforgettable. (When we make this trip by caravan we'll send Mom and Dad by plane as far as Cuzco and then we'll do this bit of the journey by road.)

We drove along, scaring off llamas and making Indian women rush to shift their shaggy donkeys, which watched us go by with an air of philosophical indifference. Suddenly all the beauties of nature were equaled, if not eclipsed, by the work of man. Before our eyes rose Ollantaytambo, a fortress built on an almost inaccessible pinnacle of rock. Blocks of granite weighing several tons had been raised to seemingly impossible heights. The construction so perfectly calculated that it serves as well for sowing maize in times of peace as it does for turning into an impregnable fortress when attacked.

Full of admiration and joy, we explored every inch of the fortress and its outposts, and even planned where we'll camp when we come back with the caravan.

We drove more slowly on our return and had a look at several very picturesque villages, including Pucuyra, Talca and Yucay, the prettiest and most welcoming, which centuries ago was a kind of Inca resort.

Everywhere we saw how Indians are exploited by whites. We realized that the parasites living in the city are taking advantage of the hard-working Indians, forcing them to sow crops higher and higher in the sierras. An Indian to whom we gave a lift explained in his modest Spanish how one particular landowner was swindling him. About ten years ago he got married and built a little house right out in the jungle at an altitude of about 2,000 feet. He spent three years chopping down the brush, burning the stubble and preparing the ground for growing crops. The landowner said nothing to him all this time, but when the crop was ready for harvesting he sent the police to turn him out. The man picked up and went, taking his wife and the two children they had by then, and moved much higher up the hillside. He spent three or four years clearing this piece of jungle and, just when he thought he was about to enjoy the fruits of his labor, the landowner had him turned out again. Pelao and I looked at each other, hardly knowing whether to be appalled or enraged in the face of such fatalistic submission. How meekly the man told the story of this immense, unpunished injustice.

Machu Picchu, 5 April 1952

We're waiting at the station for the train that will take us back to Cuzco and the twentieth century. I'm still overwhelmed by all that I've seen, aware of how little we know of our native America and of how prophetic Fúser's words turned out to be when he told me in Zapala, "Heads or tails, Petiso. It's all heads or tails."

I'm going to go back over the events of the last few days. We set out for Machu Picchu on the 3rd. The terrain is so steep that the railway has to climb in a zigzag, working like a funicular. Part of the way the locomotive pushes the wagons, part of the way it pulls them. The track runs along beside the Pomatales, a tributary of the Vilcanota. The higher you go, the more tropical and lush the vegetation becomes; the hillsides are covered with broom and the foot of the mountain with capulíes laden with fruit. We passed through several villages—Pucuyra, Iracuchaca, Huacondo and others. In each we were assaulted by Indian women offering us plates of food. There was steaming corn on the cob, fragrant goat cheeses and cassava covered in hot sauces, which smelled exotic to us.

Soon the Pomatales flows into the Vilcanota. The mountains all around become higher and steeper. Custard-apple trees appear, as well as toroc and lots of different ferns and the most beautiful begonias. (My mother and Maso would have filled the caravan with plants by now.) The river grows steadily into a raging torrent and one series of rapids follows another, with waves whose crests are several yards high, causing the tremendous sound that the Indians call the Great Roar.

We got out onto the platform in Machu Picchu and headed for the ruins, five miles higher up. We followed an old mule-track, which is steeper but shorter than the road.

We reached a hotel near the ruins. It was empty, a good

omen for us. The man in charge was playing soccer with a few of the employees and neighbors on a little leveled area, which they call a pampas here. We asked if we could play and they let us join in, rather surprised by our arrival. When the game was over we introduced ourselves. The man in charge is a writer, maybe one of those left-wingers who had to disappear to evade persecution under Odría.[2] He got the measure of us at once and, seeing we weren't as short of intelligence and knowledge as we were of clothes and money, he offered us free board and lodgings.

We went out to look round the ruins. The landscape alone is worth the trip. The buildings are all of white granite and stand on a promontory about 2,000 feet above the river, which runs through a narrow gorge flanked by high hills, some of which are covered in snow. It was dusk, and a few low clouds were gradually covering the peaks, as if shrouding them in gray gauze. A few threads of water tumbling down in graceful cascades completed this wonderful spectacle.

But if nature presents a spectacle of grandeur here, the work of man in no way lags behind. Sheltered in the shadow of Huayna Picchu lies one of the greatest works of the indigenous civilizations of South America.

The summit of Machu Picchu, which gave its name to the city (thought to be the ancient Vilcapampa), is surrounded on three sides by the River Vilcanota. The only way in is by a path approaching from the south. I shall describe the fortress starting from there, where you come first to a watchtower or outpost, built of blocks of white granite, which could hold ten to twelve men. From there you go down to the area that comprises the royal city proper. The Sun Temple dominates the Eastern Valley, rising up over a cave cut into the living rock, which must

[2] Manuel A. Odría (1897–1974), Peruvian dictator who was President from 1950 to 1956.

have been the royal mausoleum. Using the same rock, they built this temple all of a piece, with granite blocks that fit together perfectly without any break in continuity. As the walls rise higher the blocks get smaller, giving the temple at once an appearance of endurance and a wonderful, delicate grace. It is semicircular in shape, which has earned it the name of The Turret among visitors. It has several windows, one of which has two sliding blocks at the bottom with cylindrical channels about two inches in diameter running through them, which is where the gold disc symbolizing the sun was fastened. We came down at nightfall. The hotel keeper invited us to dinner.

Before going to sleep I was reading a book that the guide lent me. It's a collection of letters written by Bolívar.[3] Profound and topical, they fired my imagination. I thought to myself that I was right to follow the imperious voice of my blood, which called me to wander through America until I found something new, where I could develop my full physical, scientific and intellectual potential.

On the 4th we got up at dawn and began the ascent of Huayna Picchu—the Young Peak, as opposed to Machu Picchu, the Old Peak. This young peak rises to some 1,200 feet above the fortress of Vilcapampa. The path is steep but easy to follow. We reached the ruins of the little fortress, took a few photos, and left a piece of paper with our signatures on it in a bottle so that we can look for it when we come back—if we ever do.

We came across a strawberry field on the way down and had ourselves a feast. That afternoon we went to the sacrifice room, which is in The Turret. We took the kettle and maté. I lit a fire, put the kettle on to boil and lay down on the sacrificial stone. My thoughts turned to the Bolívar letters I read last night. Fúser sat on a rock nearby

[3] Simón Bolívar (1783–1830), Venezuelan general and statesman who liberated seven countries of South America from Spanish rule.

and prepared the maté while reading a book by Bingham,[4] the rediscoverer of Machu Picchu.

I came out of my reverie and said to Ernesto, "You know what I'm going to do? I'm going to marry María Magdalena. Since she's a descendant of Manco Capac II, I'll become Manco Capac III. Then I'll form a pro-Indian party, I'll take all these people to the coast to vote, and that'll be the start of the new Tupac Amaru revolution, the American Indian revolution!"

Ernesto looked at me and listened with seriousness unwarranted by my humorous outburst, and once again he surprised me with one of his powerful verdicts. "Revolution without firing a shot? You're crazy, Petiso."

I wrote all of the above sitting on a suitcase. The journey back is much slower than the journey out. The train spends more time standing still than moving. People get on and off to pick ñucchu flowers for the procession on Monday. We left the wonder of the Inca civilization nine hours ago, and there's still no hope of reaching Cuzco. I've spent the time thinking about the beauty I've seen, about all I've learned and about how much I still have to learn.

Thinking about the poverty of these people, half hidden behind the steam rising from their cooking pots of soup as they struggle to earn a few coins for their children, and about what Pelao said. I can't get his words out of my mind. "Revolution without firing a shot? You're crazy, Petiso."

When you come down to it, it's very much like what he answered back almost ten years ago, when we asked secondary-school pupils to hold a protest demonstration to call for the release of hundreds of university students who had been arrested. That was in December 1943. I had taken part in the Córdoba University student strike when

[4] *The Lost City of the Incas* by American archaeologist Hiram Bingham (1875–1956), who rediscovered Machu Picchu in 1911.

the university was seized under orders from General Farrel's[5] *de facto* government. I'd been arrested along with every other member of the student union.

While I was held, my brothers brought me food, which we pooled with supplies brought in by other students' relatives and by the strike committee to offset the swill we were given at the police station where we were held without trial. Ernesto had come along with my brother on one of these trips. While the food was handed over we were given ten minutes' visiting time. I took the opportunity to get across the idea that we'd already given a number of visitors—to organize the high-school students to call for our release or at least for us to be handed over to the courts. Up until then we had simply been abducted; we weren't listed anywhere as being under arrest.

When I finished my plea, my brother Tomás said he thought it was a good idea, but Pelao came out with one of his typical ripostes, saying, "Go out and march unarmed so they can beat the shit out of us? Not on your life. I'm not going without a piece."

Ten years on the outlook is the same—the revolution is won with gunfire. Two different periods, but a single attitude to life.

---

[5] Edelmiro J. Farrel (1887–1980), Argentine general and *de facto* President of Argentina from 1944 to 1946.

To the Huambo leprosarium

Cuzco, 6 April 1952

Today we attended the inauguration ceremony for one of the restored cathedral towers destroyed by the 1950 earthquake. The tower holds one of the biggest bells in the world, the María Angola. They say there is a great deal of gold in the bell, which makes its peal more resonant.

The most interesting thing—for us, anyway—was that instead of playing the Spanish Royal March, the band played the Hymn of the Spanish Republic. The desperate attempts of the Spanish consul to shut them up were a sight to see. Pelao and I fell about laughing and came to the conclusion that this was the revenge of Tupac Amaru and the Quechua and Spanish peoples against the Church and Franco's fascists.

That afternoon we went back to see Sacsa Huaman again. Without a doubt it is as great a fortress as Machu Picchu, but unfortunately, being so near to hand, there was nothing to stop the Spaniards taking the stones that formed its walls to build their own churches. The fortress consists of two sections; in one stands the throne of the Inca. There are flights of stairs up to the throne, some of which have three or more steps carved out of a single block of granite. The other section has several fountains and a semicircular building that held the Intihuatana, or House of the Sun.

There are blocks that weigh more than a ton, and the

most typical and wonderful thing about them is the way they interlock. There are several theories about this, including the version that this method of arranging them meant that, if a stone was removed, it could be replaced by another without affecting the stability of the wall. Some of these stones have as many as twelve facets. At Machu Picchu they showed us one with thirty-two.

One of the legends says that the Incas handled stone easily because they knew of a herb whose juice could soften the stone like clay. There is a bird that nests in the rock, our informant tells us. It can do so because it too is familiar with this herb and carries some in its beak to make a hollow in the rock for its nest.

It's a very nice legend, but Pelao and I agree that man's labor and ingenuity are the juice that softens the stone so that such wonders can be built.

We ate in the market today, where we asked for that strange stew they call ajiaco and serve on maize or cabbage leaves by way of a plate. Afterward we went to see the procession of the Lord of the Earthquakes. It's a real pagan festival; you almost expect the Quechuas to take off their ponchos and start dancing round the statue, shouting and whooping with their hands over their mouths as in Hollywood films.

The figure of Christ, made out of dark paste, which gave it a dark coppery color, was being borne along by some downtrodden Indians followed by a rowdy army band. Behind them came a series of officials of varying degrees of importance, and behind them a great crowd of ragged Indians, with the women carrying their children on their backs, and all talking and chewing their coca or their corncobs while the ñucchu flowers meant for Christ floated down about their heads.

The inhabitants of Cuzco followed the procession, either compelled by their masters or out of the fear sown in their minds by the priests, but the Indians' attitude makes me think that they believe in this Christ as much as Fúser and I do.

Abancay, 11 April 1952
We're beside a stream that runs through one of the town's many gullies. The place is almost like Eden, with a warm but not tropical climate. The stream widens into a pool, where one can swim, and medlars and fig trees give us shade and fruit. The only things missing are Eve and the serpent, especially Eve.

But I'll go back to our last few days in Cuzco. After getting a letter of introduction from Dr. Hermosa for the doctor running the leprosarium at Huambo, and having made a strategic retreat from María Magdalena's hearth and home, we started the necessary organizational maneuvers to continue our journey. We spent several days making determined efforts—and waiting. We put up at the National Guard barracks.

They put us in the same room as an officer under arrest, who turned out to be worthy of our gallery of unbelievable individuals. He is considerably better educated than the average officer, has a far-reaching imagination and is imbued with the same imperialist spirit as more or less the entire Peruvian military. We discussed various subjects, but kept coming back to the annexation psychosis of the Peruvian soldier.

He tried to convince us that Peru ought to go to war against Chile. And as if that weren't enough, he was so far removed from reality that he talked about bombing the centers of production and paralyzing the hydroelectric power stations. We answered, "What do you mean paralyze?" Chile's arms and munitions are imported from the USA, and all the power stations do is provide dim lighting for a few streets—they don't supply any major industry.

Besides, to do this Peru would need planes capable of fly-ing 2,500 or more miles—which their Yankee masters have never sold them and won't allow them to have.

Not only did we refute all his arguments, we also brought him face to face with the fact that, instead of hon-oring the heroes of the Liberation, they devote themselves to singing the praises of two or three generals who were defeated in their fratricidal war against their Chilean brothers.

After this last discussion we tried not to talk with him much. I spent the time reading in the library, while Fúser went back to the museum, which I avoided for the reasons hinted at above.

When they chucked me out of the library I would go back to the barracks and read the only interesting book I found there—Merezhkovski's *Napoleon*. It's not as good as his *Leonardo da Vinci*, but it's readable and throws light on certain aspects of Bonaparte's character that were unknown to me.

At last we managed to get transport on a vehicle leav-ing for Abancay, which is on the way to Huambo. As usual the road presented us with some magnificent surprises. It climbs continuously from Cuzco until it gets to a place called Abra. We started up a snow-covered peak, and after a few minutes we were driving along on a high plateau, which is at the same altitude as the snow-covered moun-taintops. At dusk we began to descend and advanced through a mist, which added a new hint of danger to our journey.

Seen from the road, the River Apurimac looked like a fine thread of water lying between little promontories, which are in fact huge hills. The route is extremely rough, full of bends that run along the edge of sheer precipices, but the landscape is so beautiful it makes you forget the danger. Later on, as the sun was going down, its last rays lit just the snow-covered summits and gave them the most beautiful glint of silver. Together with the grandeur of the hills, with their cloud-covered summits, it brought home to me the fact that beauty has no limits.

The moon came out as we began the descent, and it created a halo round the highest hilltops. For several hundred yards along the road, clouds lay below us. We drove along at a dizzying speed, experiencing the rare phenomenon of traveling under skies that were alternately clear and cloudy.

We reached Abancay, and in less than an hour we had gone from the near-polar cold of Abra to the hot climate of the valley. We introduced ourselves at the hospital. They invited us to dinner, and right afterward we went to bed.

Today, 11 April, we rested for a while in the gully and then went back to the hospital. We had lunch, washed our clothes and gave the nurses a little talk on clinical laboratory methods. As on other occasions, we ended up talking about the adventures of the journey, and in the end we each went off, chatting and flirting with a nurse.

We met again at dusk and had a look round the town, ending up at the stream. Lying on my back gazing at the sky, I tried to think over some of the things that have happened, but I couldn't drift away because the scene before me was so beautiful I could do nothing other than admire it. Before my eyes the sky turned from pale blue to a pearly shade of pink that grew fainter and fainter. To my left the mountain chain surrounded by its eternal retinue of clouds turned a steadily darkening bluish-gray. If I tipped my head back a little I could see a patch of sky that was still blue, cut into whimsical shapes by the eucalyptus trees growing on the banks of the rushing stream. The first stars began to twinkle, and a whole symphony of colors melted into a single shade of gray.

We started back. After a brief debate, since I wanted to

return the same way we had come and Fúser was all for taking a shortcut across the hillside, we took a path chosen at random. It soon disappeared into the undergrowth and we began climbing up in the dark, looking for the road that runs along the top of the ravine.

The climb got harder and harder, and we had to grab onto brambles and trees to haul ourselves up, until at last we reached a cultivated patch and then a stone wall. We climbed over it and found ourselves face to face with the farmer, who must have regarded us as a couple of demons, since he took to his heels crying out, "Viracocha!" several times as he went. We caught up with him and explained that we were trying to reach the road. Having recovered his composure, he showed us the way.

As we were approaching the town we came upon the strange spectacle of a long column of torches, which turned out to be the Maundy Thursday procession—a long line of girls from Catholic schools and the local God-squad.

When we got back to the hospital we gave a lecture on leprosy and asthma, as a corollary to which Ernesto had a brutal attack and had to have two injections of adrenalin almost one after another.

Huancarama, 13 April 1952

As the doctors recommended by Dr. Hermosa know nothing about leprosy and have no interest in our visiting the leprosarium, we decided to continue on our way under our own steam.

We got a truck to bring us to this little town, where I have had a major scare. We had barely arrived when I had to give Pelao an injection for a fierce asthma attack, to which he was psychologically predisposed since there isn't a general clinic or a pharmacy anywhere in town and we had only a single vial of adrenalin left.

At about four o'clock in the morning Ernesto woke me up in desperation; his asthma attack had intensified again. As we had no adrenalin we decided that I should give him an intravenous injection of calcium chloride in order to cause him stress, which would stimulate his own adrenal medulla to secrete adrenalin.

I went out into the street, collected a little water from the stream running past the farmhouse where we had put up that night, used it to sterilize the needle and the syringe, and gave him the injection. He calmed down a bit, and I fell asleep.

Suddenly I was woken by moans. I lit a match, and the sight of Ernesto made me leap to my feet. He looked as if he were in the throes of an attack of tetanus. His whole body was arched off the ground, supported only by his neck and heels, and his mouth and face were contracted. These signs, known as opisthotonos and trismus, are characteristic of tetanus.

I didn't know what to do. It occurred to me that the water in the spring must have contained tetanic spores, which could have caused the attack. But then I thought: No, that was impossible in such a short time. Fortunately, the contraction eased, Ernesto's body gradually resumed a normal position and his moaning gave way to snoring which, however annoying I may have found it in the past, last night sounded like heavenly music to my ears.

After such a bad night, we got up late and negotiated with the town "governor" to get hold of a couple of horses to take us to Huambo. The horses were brought at about eleven in the morning, but to tell the truth I'm not sure they deserved the name. They were the size of a common donkey and so thin they looked as if they would never take our weight.

With a young Indian leading the way, we set out for

Huambo. The animals adopted a pace slower than that of a man, and didn't change speed once during the whole trip.

With his satchel and his leather jacket and his long legs, Fúser was the spitting image of the hero of Benito Lynch's[1] novel *El inglés de los güesos*, while my excess weight— loaded down with the knapsack and the blankets—made my poor nag snort with effort.

To reach Huambo you have to skirt a series of hills covered with vegetation and adorned with the golden flowers of broom and many other species unknown to me. The path is very rough, sometimes following the edge of vast precipices, with the river snaking its way along the bottom, and sometimes descending to water level and crossing over. Sometimes we went through desolate areas, and sometimes we passed Indians who, as it happens, began their Easter celebrations yesterday. These celebrations last a week, during which everybody—men, women and even children—drinks chicha, a maize liquor, and cane brandy, and they dance to the rhythm of their various drums, panpipes and flutes until alcohol and weariness overcome them and they end up sprawling in some corner of their hut, or on the edge of the road, if sleep happened to overtake them just as they went out to visit a friend.

So as we went through the various little villages we were accompanied by sounds of the Indians' festivities. The way began to seem long and it grew steadily rougher; sometimes it seemed to climb up and down veritable flights of steps in the rock, and only the horses we rode, being small and used to the terrain, were capable of following the path without losing their footing.

During all this time a couple of Indians followed us as we went along—a middle-aged woman and a boy, the same

---

[1] Benito Lynch (1885–1951), Argentine writer whose famous novel *El inglés de los güesos (The Englishman with the Bones)* contrasts the European spirit with that of the local criollo.

one who had helped us at the beginning of our march. From time to time they spoke to us in Quechua, but as the woman was carrying several baskets we thought they were offering us something for sale and paid them no attention.

After we had been riding for about three hours, and after crossing a series of hills thinking each one was the last, we finally came out into a valley. We found ourselves on a plateau, with a vast ravine stretching away to our right, flanked by two mountain ranges, parts of which were under cultivation. There was a patchwork of varied greenery, overlooked by a red-roofed estate, behind and above which we could see the rest of the mountain covered in what looked like impenetrable forest. Far away in the distance to our left, Huambo had come into sight at last.

As we paused there for a moment our escorts came up to us, and the little Indian explained in rudimentary Spanish that one of these horses belonged to him and the other to the poor old woman, and that the lieutenant governor had taken them away from them and they were following us so that, when we reached our destination, they could then go back to their own homes with their horses. They lived near Abancay, which is to say several miles from where we started—but in the opposite direction.

Deeply distressed at having involuntarily been the cause of so much disrespect to a fellow human being, we dismounted and restored the horses to their owners. To assuage our pangs of conscience we gave them a sol and offered to take a photo of them. The little Indian posed for the camera with a huge smile, but the descendant of Mama Oello was satisfied with having recovered her horse and headed off downhill along a little path that went toward the gully, without waiting for any other compensation.

We continued on foot, talking about the ignominious

Alberto Granado (left) with his brother Tomás and La Poderosa II
in November 1949 at San Francisco del Chañar, Córdoba,
Argentina. *(Photographs courtesy of Lucía Álvarez de Toledo)*

(Right to left) Ernesto Guevara, Gregorio Granado, Alberto Granado, Tomas Granado, Nery Cambronero, and Alberto Prato after a rugby match in Córdoba, 1950.

Alberto Granado (right) and his brother Gregorio with Ernesto Guevara on his bike in 1950.

Minutes before leaving home in Córdoba, 1951, Alberto
Granado (left) says goodbye to his brothers Gregorio and Tomás.

At Lake Nahuel Huapi in Southern Argentina.

Alberto Granado (front left) and Ernesto Guevara (center, with cap) with La Poderosa II shortly before leaving it in Santiago, Chile

Alberto Granado peeling potatoes and onions on board the *San Antonio*, sailing from Valparaíso to Antofagasta in Chile, 1952.

Cuzco, Peru

Alberto Granado (left) and personnel from the San Pablo
Leprosarium fishing in the Amazon River.
(Photo taken by Ernesto Guevara)

Alberto Granado (left) and Ernesto Guevara on board the
Mambo Tango raft on the Amazon in 1952.

behavior of those who think they have the power to rule over people's lives and property just because they hold official positions.

We stopped for a break in the shade of a prickly pear tree, and since it was laden with fruit we satisfied both our hunger and thirst by stuffing ourselves. A few minutes later, at the end of a shaded and soggy path where the sun's rays couldn't penetrate the dense foliage of the capulíes, we stood ankle-deep in mud, facing the leprosarium of Huambo.

It is difficult to describe what I felt when I saw the leprosarium. Although the huts we had seen along the way—and, above all, the fact that it was so removed from civilization—had prepared me for something inadequate for its purpose, everything I had imagined paled beside the reality. I glanced at Fúser, and from the look on his face I could see he was having similar thoughts.

The so-called hospital was divided into two main parts. As with most establishments of this kind, one part is known as the healthy zone. This is where the workers carry out their duties. It consisted of a couple of rooms, with an area of about fifty square feet, mud walls and a thatched roof. One room serves as a dispensary, dining area, and as an office for administration and admissions. The other does duty as a pharmacy, consulting room, infirmary and records office. Even if the inventor of order existed, he could never have put order into these two rooms, so we weren't shocked to see swabs on the floor, vials of sulfetrona in one corner and patients' medical histories in another, with a jumble of aprons and surgical gloves hanging from a nail. Generally speaking, everything was neat considering the circumstances.

The staff comprises one head health worker and three male nurses. They gave us a very friendly reception and suggested we visit the patients the next day. Today they're going to put us up at a nearby estate, because the sanatorium has no amenities.

Huambo, 14 April 1952

Today we saw the other part of the hospital, the patients' section. If we got a sorry impression of where the staff work, the area where the patients stay gave us an even sorrier one. The two parts were divided by a wall, and the patients' part is made up of four wings. Each of these was made up of several windowless mud huts, and each of the three huts that comprise each wing housed four patients. The poor patients were vegetating on mattresses made of reeds in these hovels, which were barely six feet high and entirely lacking in sanitary or hygienic facilities.

A little farther off is a patch of ground enclosed within an adobe wall, where the patients able to manage for themselves alleviate their boredom by planting cassava, potatoes, ocumos and maize. This is all there is to the Huambo leprosarium.

Just as we were returning from our tour a new arrival entered the admissions office. She was quite a young woman, originally from Iquitos, who had been diagnosed in Cuzco as suffering from leprosy. When she found herself in this poky little excuse for a room she could not help giving in to a fit of complete and quite justified despair. We tried to console her with a few friendly words, and sat on the edge of the bed as paternally as possible, trying to convince her that if she accepted the treatment, she would be able to go home fairly soon. We left her somewhat consoled.

Then we went to see another patient, a former teacher at a nearby school. She was very moved when we greeted her with a handshake and sat on the same chairs she sat on, and her tears—a blend of sorrow and happiness—moved us too. We had our picture taken with her and went on with our tour.

The visit presented us with yet another sad surprise. In the last of the huts are four children, all under six, living with their parents, who are suffering from lepromatous leprosy. We checked whether the children had been given a BCG[2] injection to increase their resistance and, of course, they hadn't. With the susceptibility they have inherited from their parents and living in continual direct contact with them, they are condemned to contract the disease themselves.

At the end of our visit some of the patients got together to show us their artistic talents. Among them was a remarkable trio, who played a kind of single-stringed violin they had made themselves.

Then we met the real anonymous heroes who are struggling to maintain the hospital and keep it running—Mr. Montejo and his three assistants, Vivanco, Montoya and Valdivia. They told us about all the shortages they suffer for want of a regular doctor, because the current doctor sometimes lets two months go by without turning up at the leprosarium.

We asked them about the children. They told us it was impossible to persuade the parents to part with them, and that if they separated them by force the parents would escape from the hospital. We asked if they had given the children a BCG injection, which, though meant to prevent tuberculosis, apparently has the capacity to create antibodies that protect the organism from Hansen's bacillus[3] as well. We were told that although there had been a great deal of talk about this, they had not been able to get the national authorities to supply them with the drug, in spite of repeated requests by Dr. Pesce, who, according to them, is the only scientist in

[2] BCG: bacillus of Calmette and Guerin, or Koch, used as inoculation against tuberculosis.
[3] Hansen's bacillus: another name for leprosy is Hansen's disease, after G. H. Hansen (1841–1912), a Norwegian doctor who discovered the leprosy bacillus.

Peru who cares about patients suffering from Hansen's disease.

Nevertheless I should say that the picture here is not entirely bleak. To begin with, the medication is up-to-date. The patients are given promanide and sulphetrone, which is currently the most effective drug against the *Mycobacterium leprae*. Ferrous sulphate is used to combat their anemia. The food is quite good and the patients supplement their diet with green vegetables they gather themselves, and for protein they eat cuises, or guinea pigs, usually used in the laboratory, which grow here to a large size and weight.

But the most outstanding thing is the way both Mr. Montejo and his assistants treat the patients with the greatest sympathy and affection, and this makes up for many of the hospital's deficiencies.

That afternoon we visited a new sanatorium that is being built a mile or so away from the old one. The road there is extremely picturesque, which is only to be expected in these parts. The track runs through a valley along the banks of a small river, then it climbs up the hillsides or crosses some farmer's maize field. Unfortunately we were pursued the whole way by mosquitoes, leaving us covered in bites and swellings. This trip would have been wonderful, but for the fact that Fúser was still feeling the effects of a bad asthma attack that he suffered last night, which eased only when I gave him two adrenalin injections.

We arrived at the new leprosarium. It is larger than the old one, but is still a long way from being an acceptable establishment. It has no operating theater, no laboratory and no common room for the patients. In short, it's a warehouse in which to store patients, with a greater capacity than the other—and nothing more.

When we set out on our way back Fúser felt his asthma

attack worsening and he had to sit down and wait while I went to fetch a syringe and some adrenalin. One of the nurses offered to go back on horseback, with the idea that this way he would get there quicker and give Fúser his injection. Approximately forty-five minutes later Ernesto appeared on the threshold, pale and gasping and almost unable to utter a word, asking me with his eyes what had happened. He and the nurse had crossed paths on the way.

When he had recovered, thanks to the effect of the injection, we went back to the estate to have dinner. This is an immense ranch stretching from here to the River Vilcanota—that is, almost to Machu Picchu. It has great areas under alfalfa, providing pasture for hundreds of cows, whose milk is industrially processed. They also grow sugar cane along the Vilcanota and distill cane brandy from the juice—a real poison and great ally to these landowners.

When the estate owner learned we were professionals, he began to treat us with great deference and friendliness and afforded us every comfort. You would never believe this same person is capable of the most inhuman exploitation of other beings, who are just as much flesh and blood as we are.

His method of obtaining arable land is the same as all these exploiters employ. He allows neighboring farmers to come and live on his property. He gives them a bit of virgin forest to settle in. They clear a patch of ground each year, manuring and cultivating it, and when the cultivated area is big enough he has them turned out. If they want to stay they have to take on another uncultivated patch higher up on the mountainside, and he keeps driving them on like this up toward the summit, where the ground is drier.

He told us all about these abusive methods over a steaming plate of chicken soup accompanied by full-bodied Chilean wines. But neither the good food nor the danger of having to sleep out in the open prevented us from criticizing these methods sharply. The man couldn't believe his ears and poor Mr. Montejo, who had introduced us, kept signaling us to shut up. Dinner came to an end at last and we went to bed.

In spite of a persistent drizzle, the two horses and the guide that the estate owner had offered us were ready at five o'clock in the morning. As we were about to leave the boss came out, still frowning, and suggested we stay until it cleared up. We thanked him for his offer, but rejected it. We went down to the leprosarium, said our goodbyes to both staff and patients and set out for Huancarama.

To the Peruvian rain forest

Huancarama, 15 April 1952

The journey was very slow because of the terrible state of the roads after the punishing rains. When we arrived we found a great number of Indians celebrating their carnival. The majority, both men and women, were drunk and playing their quena flutes and dancing yaravíes and carnavalitos. The women, probably because of the alcohol, were much bolder than usual and, perhaps shocked by our attire, shouted to us and made obscene gestures, but it was nothing to get worked up about.

We reached the town at about four in the afternoon. Pelao was having a really bad asthma attack. We went to the Civil Guard post, but it was deserted. The police too were out on a binge. Ernesto collapsed in a corner, while I went out to look for water to sterilize the syringe. I bumped into a woman, asked her for water, and to my surprise she said she'd been looking for me. She had heard that two doctors were in town and wanted us to look at her sick father. She virtually dragged me, and I had no choice but to go and examine the man. As I did, a group of people with sick children turned up. I wrote prescriptions for the medicines they might find in the leprosarium pharmacy—the only place nearby to obtain medicine. Then I asked for water to sterilize the syringe.

The water they gave me was earth-colored and looked polluted. It would need to be boiled for quite a while.

Fortunately it began to rain, so I threw this water away and filled the pot with rainwater. When I returned nearly an hour later Fúser was quite desperate, not knowing what might have been keeping me. As I boiled the syringe, I told him what had happened. I injected him with a vial and a half of coramina that the hospital had given us. After a few minutes the beneficial effect of the adrenalin had put him to sleep.

Andahuaylas, 16 April 1952
This town is large enough to have a hospital, so we'll be able to get some treatment for Ernesto.

The road here, like all the others in the region, rose and fell sharply. At midday the driver of the truck we rode in stopped for lunch at a farmhouse. We had resigned ourselves to fasting, but our fame preceded us the mile or so up to the farm and we were summoned for a consultation. I examined a healthy child and a woman who probably has a tumor on one of her ovaries. So I prescribed nothing for the child and said that the woman should see a specialist in the city. They invited me to sit down to lunch with them and sent Fúser two plates of boiled potatoes and a plate of mote, as boiled maize is called around here.

Despite his asthma, Fúser ate well. The remains we shared with some little Indians who stared at us while we ate. It seems impossible that such cheerful, playful and charming children after a couple of years of ill-treatment, contempt and religion will be rendered unfit to be anything more than servants. To cap it all, chewing coca and drinking cane brandy makes them mistrustful, lazy and submissive.

By the time we reached the town, Ernesto was having another attack. We had to stop in a garage, where they allowed me to sterilize the syringe. After dosing him with adrenalin again and making him lie down on a bench, I

went in search of lodgings. After a few unsuccessful forays
I met a man called Romero. He patiently accompanied me
to all the bars and brothels to look for the doctor and hospital manager, and managed to get us a room at the hospital. That evening he invited us to supper.

Andahuaylas, 17 April 1952

Mid-morning the doctor came to see Fúser. Clearly the
man knew little about general medicine and even less
about asthma. Unwillingly, he authorized a further night's
stay. We lunched there. The quality and quantity of the
food were unlikely to turn out healthy patients.

We met the German doctor who runs the WHO
chickenpox eradication campaign. He promised to take us
to Huanta in his van.

Andahuaylas, 18 April 1952

Today we went to thank the garage owner for his help.
When he learned of Dr. Montes's unhelpful manner he
offered us what little he had. As in Argentina and Chile,
here in Peru it's the poorest people who are generous. The
better-off in general, and doctors in particular, are loath to
show the slightest humanity. And they call themselves
doctors! Usually, as with this Montes, they are the sons of
millionaires who get rich exploiting the Indians. The title
"Doctor" is but an adornment to increase their wealth,
not a means to alleviate the suffering of humanity.

Andahuaylas, 19 April 1952

We spent all today at the police station, because the doctor threw us out of the hospital. We decided to skip the
barracks cuisine and instead cooked up some potatoes,
maize and ocumo. In the afternoon we brewed maté and
we had to ask the prisoners for something to boil the
water in, so we got talking to them. Most are soldiers

driven to desertion by homesickness. With flawless logic they think it absurd to spend three years running errands for officers and their wives or mistresses while their plots of land become rank with weeds.

As we sipped our maté I noticed that the maté gourd had cracked. We applied adhesive tape to it, but to no avail. I went to get a rag from my bag so as not to burn my fingers and there I came across a handkerchief embroidered by my mother. It brought back a flood of memories. I told Pelao that once we stopped wandering and were back home sipping maté, we'd remember this maté shared with prisoners and deserters in the midst of fighting off the artful attack of bedbugs.

The peaceful moment was brief. The prison is housed in the police headquarters, and it was visiting day. Long lines of Indians, mostly prisoners' wives, were waiting to enter. They were accompanied by their children, goats and even donkeys. Each visitor had to be searched. One of the guards, in a repulsive abuse of his authority, did much more than frisk them. He groped their breasts and thighs and gloated as he touched their genitals. Not even a ten-year-old Indian girl escaped his lewdness. For us it was really the last straw.

Together we strode toward the guard to call him to order, but the sergeant, who was sitting nearby, was openly enjoying his subordinate's antics. Fúser and I looked at each other helplessly, gathered up our things and left.

Ayacucho, 22 April 1952

The 19th found us dejectedly ruminating on our impotence when confronted with the abuse of authority against those poor Indian girls. But we were saved by the providential appearance of a worker, a representative of man's true potential, the creator of wealth that others enjoy, he who must one day rule this beautiful world so badly governed at present.

As I was saying, we came across a poor worker from a neighboring farm who offered us supper and a corner to sleep. The following day he organized a truck to take us to Huancayo. First we went to Huanta and at nightfall, around eight o'clock, we continued on to Huancayo. The night trip was no different from others. The Indians settled themselves as best they could, and we ended up sleeping head to toe with them. Fortunately my olfactory nerve soon closed down and I slept.

Around midnight we passed through Ayacucho. We were told that a landslide had blocked the road, so this famous city, which sealed Spain's defeat in the Americas, was our abode last night and today.

The Ayacucho–Las Mercedes road, 23 April 1952

By two o'clock we were watching a tractor clearing the rubble from the road. Three dynamite charges were used to shift the huge boulder blocking the way.

We went for a swim in the nearby River Mautaro while we waited. The road was cleared by six, and on we went. We had barely gone a mile or two when we came upon another landslide, but this time it was loose earth. The drivers, assistants and passengers set to and quickly the road became passable again. "It's true that unity is strength," Pelao remarked, "but it has to be the strength of the working people. If anyone had said that they would not wield a pick or a spade, that unity would have broken. Surely this would have been the case if, instead of a convoy of peasants, truck drivers and oddballs like us, some of the professionals we have met over the last few days had been here."

Agreeing with his words, I noted them down.

On we traveled. The road became very steep. As we climbed, the temperature dropped. At 2 a.m. the cold was quite unbearable. My feet were frozen and numb, so I took

off my boots—no easy task in that crowded pile of bodies—and rubbed them vigorously. That was how we
arrived in Huancayo, our present resting place.

La Merced, 25 April 1952

Yesterday afternoon we entered what people here call the
mountains. It's really only a forested high plateau. The
Huancayo–Palca road is like all the others we've traveled,
but the Palca–La Merced is far more dangerous.

Before leaving Palca we witnessed a sort of carnival
parade—mostly women with masks dancing to violins,
drums and panpipes, practicing for the May festival.

Before leaving we had several drinks of maize liquor
with the driver, which put us in a happy mood. The mood
evaporated, however, a few miles farther on as we found
ourselves going round hairpin bends and down a road so
narrow that passing vehicles virtually grazed each other.
On one of the bends the driver carried out a spine-chilling
maneuver on the brink of the abyss to pass another truck.
At one point a wheel of our vehicle hung out over the
edge. Five or six hundred feet below rushed a river.

Just before coming in to La Merced, the road straight-
ened and entered a real forest. Hundreds of acres of it were
cultivated, however, with orange, banana and avocado
groves. The climate has changed from the dry cold of a few
hours ago into humid heat.

We couldn't find lodgings. Finally a guesthouse offered
us a bed for the modest price of two soles, including a cup
of hot chocolate and bread. We hadn't eaten for two days
and our bellies were beginning to protest. Fortunately we
spied some orange trees through the window, so we filled
the empty hole with fruit.

La Merced, 26 April 1952

Today we visited the malaria hospital. We gave a brief talk

on leprosy and on the anti-malaria drive being carried out in Tucumán, in Argentina. Afterward we were invited to a meal and we ate sumptuously.

That afternoon we set out for Oxapampa. The road, as windy as ever, passed between small hills, but now the slopes were covered with valuable woods, such as cedar, oak, mahogany and so forth. There were also coffee and banana plantations and huge stands of avocado trees, tall papayas and leafy mangoes.

We had supper in San Luis. A man at our table appeared to be a perfectly even racial mix: 50 percent of his features were Spanish and 50 percent African. He was a small-scale farmer from a nearby city. In his own words he was proud of his "pleasant, cultured conversation," which essentially consists of piling up ten adjectives in a single sentence. We began to mimic him, summoning up the most far-fetched words we could think of, quietly mocking his colloquial virtues. Initially he took us for a pair of complete liars. However, with time and as we replied honestly and to the best of our knowledge to his questions, he began to calm down and in the end was using no adjectives at all.

Between Oxapampa and San Ramón, 27 April 1952

The remainder of last night's journey was through rain forest. The roadside was thick with tall trees hung with lianas and beautiful climbing plants that should be displayed in an exhibition.

The recent rainfall had made the road virtually impassable. It took us twelve hours to travel the fifty miles between La Merced and Oxapampa. But for me the journey was wonderful. I feel elated here in the tropics, having always dreamed of this.

After a short nap under the truck we reached Oxapampa round about 2 a.m. At eight we went to visit the family of a dear Peruvian friend, Dávalos, who studies with my brothers at Córdoba University.

I hoped to find letters from home waiting for me, as this was one of the few pre-fixed places we planned to visit, come what may. But nothing had arrived, and despite Dávalos's sister and her husband's lavish hospitality and pleas for us to stay, I was determined to continue on to Lima.

By chance, a neighbor was leaving for Tarma that afternoon, so we fell in with him. Before leaving we visited the town, which sits in a small wooded valley. The climate is much more agreeable here than in La Merced, and there is no malaria.

All the houses are built of cedar or oak, attractively constructed, but with an obvious absence of town planning. On the lower slopes coffee, oranges and bananas are grown. Higher up are maize, sweet potato and, in between, rice. It is a very fertile area, but the production is haphazard, and there are no roads to get the produce out. The ever-present two-sided coin!

San Ramón, 28 April 1952

On arrival, our driver suddenly announced he could not continue and left us standing in the middle of the main square of the town at two in the morning.

His strange behavior took us by surprise, but we set off toward a light in one of the few illuminated corners of the town and there we found a trio of night owls, drunk as skunks, who had quite a scare when they saw us appear in our leather jackets, with our knapsacks and bags. They must have thought we were the vanguard of an army of Martians.

Recovering from the shock, and having convinced them that we weren't paratroopers or anything of the kind, they offered us a drink. Soon we were conversing like old friends. Later on more drunks appeared, this time a duo. After brief greetings we all began singing a series of tangos and waltzes at the top of our voices.

When the bar closed we were taken to another, and we continued to drink beer and emit sounds that approximated the tango. Fúser and I employed all our skill to indicate to our hosts that we were more hungry than thirsty. As our hints went unheeded, Fúser ordered a generous portion of bread and cheese, which we devoured. As one might expect, although we tried to pay for it they wouldn't hear of it, and the amount went to swell our hosts' already rather large bill. Dawn overtook us there amid our beer and tango.

We said goodbye to our fortuitous and cordial friends and went to sleep in a derelict house which, according to the townspeople, is haunted, but not a single ghost came to disturb our slumber. Pangs of hunger we did feel, however, as our stomachs can't be fooled for long by liquid and tidbits of cheese.

In our search for something solid to eat we crossed the river. As we rubbed the sleep from our eyes we realized that the fortunate townspeople had had the excellent idea of planting orange and grapefruit trees on the river banks. Further, it had not occurred to them that they might need wire fences or any other newfangled invention, which only serve to blight the landscape.

So two hours later, after having eaten more than four dozen oranges and a dozen grapefruit each, we left, blissfully happy. But not for long. Our gastric juices were triggered off, followed even more violently by our glomeruli, and soon that incredible feast turned into a little vitamin C and a lot of urine.

At midday we had a delicious lunch—maté with bread and bread with maté.

Tarma, 30 April 1952

Yesterday at around five in the afternoon we got a lift on a truck to Tarma, once again over horrifyingly dangerous roads. This road was even narrower than the one between Palta and San Ramón, which is really saying something. We passed at least thirty crosses marking the places where trucks had gone hurtling into the abyss below, taking the lives of all their passengers with them.

As the road climbed, the ravine deepened. The road was actually carved into the hillside. If a vehicle went off the road, it wouldn't fall onto the road below, but plummet directly into the river below, as the highway formed a spiral of ascending breadth.

Suddenly the driver hit a pothole in the middle of the road. When we asked why he hadn't avoided it, he confessed that for some time his eyesight had not been good. This did not exactly allay our fears about his driving skills.

It was night when we reached Quillabamba, where we dined on milky coffee, the only food we could come by. Despite the grumbling of our stomachs, we went to sleep in the truck's cab. It was quite cold.

Ernesto cannot tell a lie

Lima, 1 May 1952

Finally we are in the capital of the viceroys. Yesterday's journey gave us a bird's-eye view of an important mining area. As one sets out from Tarma the countryside loses its tropical feel and by La Oroya we were again in hill country. Once more the high plains, the puna blanketed in scrub and the striking herds of llamas, used as pack animals carrying many sacks of all sorts of varieties of potatoes.

We continued up to about 15,000 feet at Ticlio, where the peaks are snow-capped.

We passed through several mining centers, but didn't visit them. The driver who gave us a lift stopped at the outskirts of the capital and we stayed there and slept in the truck.

El Rancho, 19 May 1952

Today we left Lima after a twenty-day stay with, on balance, a favorable impression of people and things encountered.

I shall not describe the city itself, but just the things that most impressed us. One was the Archaeological and Anthropological Museum, the work of Dr. Tello. The beauty of the artifacts from the different civilizations of the ancient Inca kingdom was quite astounding. For example, the Paracas' skill with textiles and the pictorial art of the Chancas, which competes easily with the grace of expression and beautiful colors of the ceramic art of the Muchick or Chimú.

The Incas were also scientifically advanced. We saw evidence of cranial trepans that had been carried out with great technique and skill, and the later growth of the bone shows that the individual lived for many years after the surgery.

We also admired the Chavín stone and a series of beautifully carved stone monoliths. We concluded that though the Incas were great architects and engineers, the coastal inhabitants were more artistic. They combined satirical eroticism with the beauty of the natural form. Many animals we know from Walt Disney cartoons could be inspired by the art of pre-Hispanic Peru. In the National Library we visited an exhibition of Italian art and another of reproductions spanning Michelangelo to Picasso.

Yet again Ernesto surprised me with the breadth of his knowledge, which he only displays at an apposite moment. Contemplating some works of modern art, I said to him, "Well, I can't tell one of these monstrosities from the next!"

He replied with that mock-seriousness he employs when he is about to show off some knowledge that nobody would ever have suspected in him, saying, "I don't agree with you. Firstly, you don't always have to understand something to like it. Secondly, if you start to really look at what you call monstrosities, you'll find you like some more than others, and I'm almost certain those will be the best." And putting on his professorial look and a feigned lecturer's voice, he went on to say, "So, young man, observe with care and then choose which you most like."

I did as he suggested, and little by little I could indeed differentiate contrast, color, form and effect. I looked, compared, analyzed and finally told him which I most liked.

In his usual kindly way, after flicking through the catalog, he said, "Well, Petiso, you're not as thick as you look! Of the five you liked, four are Picasso and one Pissarro, who as you know is one of the great Impressionist masters, whose surname is written with s and not a z—like that man who colonized these poor Incas."

Another interesting visit was to San Marcos, the doyen of South American universities. We found quite a revolutionary hubbub there, particularly in the Faculty of Law, the only department with an organized student body. The rest of the students have let the government sow disorder in their ranks. Thus they are prevented from becoming a political force able to channel public opinion, which is generally opposed to the existing regime.

We visited several hospitals, including the Guía, which is also a leprosarium. Finally, Dr. Hugo Pesce, whom I have left to last on purpose, because I want to speak at length about him. He is the most important person we have met on the journey so far.

People had spoken of him in Huambo and in Cuzco, and I had a letter of introduction to him from Dr. Argüello Pitt, so we went to meet him as soon as we arrived in Lima. We hardly looked like scientists. Fúser was in his mechanic's overalls and worn, patched leather jacket, and I in my once-white trousers and leather jacket, smeared with grease and dust like some heroic scars acquired in our combats with the road.

Neither could we make up for our wretched appearance with the wealth of our scientific knowledge, as he obviously knew far more than we did. Nevertheless, he treated us with great courtesy and offered his help, using his influence to get us free lodgings in the Guía Hospital despite firm opposition from the nuns in charge. His assistant Zoraida Boluarte saw to it that we settled in comfortably. To top it all, he invited us to dine with him nearly every night.

Fúser dubbed him the Maestro, and he really is one. In every conversation we had with him we learned something, whether it was about leprosy, physiology, politics or philosophy. Through him we not only discovered César Vallejo, that great poet who spoke with the true voice of the Inca race, but also became acquainted with the physiology of the high-plains Indians.

He has various disciples, and I think he coddles them a bit. But in their work one could see the firm hand of the teacher gently guiding his inexpert pupils until they became sure of themselves. Politically he is a Marxist and has great sensitivity, as well as great dialectical ability in discussion and in dealing with problems. He has shown us that although environment makes a man, man can change it.

He'd been forced to leave Lima and his Chair in Tropical Medicine on account of being a member of the Communist Party. He settled in Andahuaylas. But instead of becoming just another regular at the numerous bars that infect that place, he devoted himself to science. He discovered endemic areas of recurring typhus where only the symptoms were known or recognized. He discovered two types of malaria-carrying mosquitoes. He discovered a source of leprosy infection and set up a center for treatment of that terrible scourge. He studied the Indian physiology. Indeed, he received and sent out so many scientific reports and papers that, according to his pupils, Andahuaylas received more correspondence than the Faculty of Medicine in Lima.

The situation became so intolerable that the government actually invited him back to his post.

He wrote a book about his experience on the high plateau called *Latitudes of Silence*. In our first days there he gave us each a copy. This led to a tragicomic scene demonstrating how uncompromisingly truthful Ernesto is.

On our last day, the Maestro invited us to a farewell dinner. I had noticed that Dr. Pesce valued Pelao's depth of knowledge on the many and varied subjects we had discussed. At the same time, Fúser regards Dr. Pesce very highly—indeed, it was his idea to call him Maestro. Which is why I value Ernesto's attitude more. But to the facts.

We arrived at the doctor's house. His wife had gone out of her way to create a sensational dinner. The first dish was Andean stew, which we attacked with gusto. After a few mouthfuls the doctor asked us, "Well, what did you think of my book? Did you like it?"

Fúser and I looked at each other. Between ourselves we had remarked on its positive and negative aspects. Our overall critique, especially Ernesto's, was not entirely favorable. I immediately answered, "It's a vivid account of the Peruvian mountains and depicts the Indian's psychology quite well."

Ernesto said nothing. The meal went on. During the dessert, the Maestro said to Pelao, "Ernesto, tell me, what is your opinion of my book?" Ernesto lifted his eyes from his plate, looked at the doctor for a few seconds and went on eating.

In the interminable silence I leaped in, saying, "By the way, I thought the description of the Urubamba flood was excellent."

His wife agreed with me and we left the matter there. But as we were leaving and after the usual farewells on the doorstep, Pesce took Ernesto's hand and returned to the attack. "You can't leave without telling me what you think of my book."

I felt a shiver run down my spine. Wagging his finger, Fúser said, "Look, Doctor, it's not a good book. The description of the landscape says nothing new, and to me

it's unbelievable that a Marxist scholar like yourself
would describe only the negative side of the Indian's psychology. It's a pessimistic book that doesn't seem to have
come from the pen of either a scientist or a Communist."

As he spoke it seemed to me that Fúser grew in stature
while Dr. Pesce shrank under Ernesto's arguments. For
what seemed an unbearable length of time, he went on
with his pointed criticism as the doctor kept nodding and
murmuring, "It's true, it's true."

So ended our farewells, and we set off to walk the forty
blocks to our lodgings. We hardly spoke until we came to
the bridge over the River Rimac. Leaning on the
balustrade, we watched the flow of dark water shimmering in the moonlight.

"Fúser, you're a shit," I said, unable to hold it in any
longer. "The poor Maestro has satisfied our hunger,
arranged our fares to San Pablo, given us money and affection and you have to throw his one weakness—his literary
pretensions—right back in his face."

"But, Mial, couldn't you see that I didn't want to say
anything?" Ernesto said, looking pained.

My anger drained away.

The next day we said goodbye to the patients in the leprosarium. We had grown quite close, we'd even played soccer with them. They gave us an envelope with a collection
of a hundred soles in it. We were very touched by their ges-
ture. In addition, one of them had put us in touch with an
army captain who owns a fleet of trucks that carry goods
from Lima to Pucallpa.

We had to contact this captain to find out where and
when we were to leave. We found him in a Masonic meeting in a Chinese restaurant in Lima's Chinatown. It was a
funny experience. We had to go through a whole rigma-
role, asking for Brother D or Brother X or Z, get past all

sorts of hurdles and closed doors, until we made it to the big boss. He was amazed we had got so far without being initiates. He told us one of his trucks was leaving on 17 May and would take us.

The Amazon and its people

On board La Cenepa *on the Ucayali River, via Iquitos, 25 May 1952*

I feel a bit low today because, apart from it being our Argentine national holiday, it is also Grego's birthday. What upsets me is not the fact of being separated from my family, but thinking that my absence may cast a shadow over the party. I hope I will be able to make it up to them by getting them to make this journey too, which has been wonderful beyond anyone's dreams.

But I shall return to the day we left Lima.

We left at about two on Sunday the 17th. The road, which runs parallel to the River Rimac, is like the one that snakes up the Chilean north coast—in other words, flanked by flat, bare hills. But as it went higher, the bleak Peruvian puna appeared again, ringed by amphitheaters of snow-capped peaks.

We retraced part of the Tarma–Lima road. Once again we drove through the Ticlio Pass, where the road peaks at around 14,000 feet, and later through the mining center of Oroya. From there we journeyed toward the Pasco Peak, crossing the Junín Plains, scene of the battle of the same name where Sucre[1] displayed his military genius and, setting a historical precedent, Argentine, Chilean, Peruvian and Venezuelan soldiers fought shoulder to shoulder.

[1] General Antonio José de Sucre (1793–1830), Venezuelan soldier-patriot who was Bolívar's lieutenant on several campaigns. He was the first President of Bolivia (1826–8).

Once more we passed by tiny Indian farms scattered through the hills. The truck did not stop that night as the two young drivers, pleasant lads nicknamed the Cambalaches, took turns driving and sleeping.

On the morning of Monday the 19th we reached Cerro de Pasco, Peru's most important mining center—in Yankee hands, of course—where gold, copper, iron and tin are extracted.

A mile or two outside Cerro de Pasco we entered a narrow valley that gradually descended, bringing us to what is called here the brow of the mountain, where the tropical vegetation begins.

At midday we came into Huanuco. After lunching we journeyed on. About fifteen miles down the road at a place called El Rancho, while traveling at top speed along the edge of a precipice, we noticed that the truck was leaning dangerously and beginning to career across the road, despite the driver's efforts to straighten it out or apply the brakes. After several hair-raising yards, and only as a result of the friction of the truck against the road surface, we came to a halt.

We jumped out and soon located the cause of the truck's strange behavior and our brush with danger. The left-wheel axle bearing had broken and shot off, making the truck suddenly swerve. We'd nearly hurtled into the abyss below.

The truck was blocking the road, so, still in shock, we had to turn ourselves to the business of shifting the vehicle. Using the branch of a tree, we levered the truck to the verge, then spent the rest of the afternoon trying to extract what remained of the pivot from the wheel. Fúser and I made occasional sorties into the thickets of fruit trees that bordered the road, to pick custard apples, luzmas and bananas.

That night we celebrated our lucky escape with three

bottles of pisco. The Cambalaches—the nickname came from the tango they're forever singing—turned out to be jolly good singers. Fúser and I, who always thought we knew a lot of tangos, were put to shame by their repertoire.

We went to bed quite merry. The next day we journeyed on.

We were in mountain country now—that is, in the forest that cloaks these hills. The road winds up and down and makes you wonder how to describe the surrounding vegetation. However much one wishes to avoid clichés, the hackneyed phrase "luxuriant foliage" springs to mind and is really a true description of the tangled profusion of trees, lianas and ferns.

The journey was extremely pleasant. The older Cambalache had gone to sleep on top of the cargo, which consisted of hundreds of sun-dried goat skins. Fúser and I sat up in the cab beside the driver, forming a trio to sing, or rather massacre, Argentine tangos and Peruvian waltzes.

My spirits are always uplifted by the rain forest and the sun. These places fill me with energy and vigor.

Such was our mood when we reached Tingo María. Some miles before we had seen the Sleeping Beauty, a mountain range that resembles a stretched-out naked woman.

The city, with its little wooden houses on stilts and surrounded by leafy trees and green lawns, is typical of the tropics. It is the season of the tea harvest and, as elsewhere in the Americas, hundreds of unemployed, many trailing their families, come looking for work as a temporary relief to their poverty. So the tea company has a plentiful labor supply.

We continued on. During the night we crossed La Aguaitía Bridge, to date the longest in South America. A

few miles along the way we had to stop owing to the
ceaseless rain, which made the road impassable.

On Thursday we went on, but slowly. We had to put
chains on the wheels against skidding.

We were in lowland rain forest. The surrounding
vegetation was increasingly lush, with saúcos, capironas,
palisangres and palos cruz all entwined in the loving arms
of creepers.

One sees only small patches of the bright red soil; the
rest is blanketed by an endless variety of grasses, ornamental leaves and ferns. Along the way we passed small
coffee, cassava and tea farms. Everywhere are stands of
banana and papaya.

Forty miles from Pucallpa we came on a huge convoy of
more than sixty trucks, detained by army order. It had
been raining in the east, and in those conditions traffic is
destructive to the roads and endangers the lives of drivers
and their passengers.

We were soon surrounded by friends of the
Cambalaches. We decided to cook a meal, even though,
unfortunately, all we had was dried meat. Pelao doesn't
often speak, but when he does he's worth listening to.
"Let's make a fire and put a piece of the meat to roast," he
said. "The smell will attract others, and we can do an
exchange." The goat meat got us pans, potatoes, spaghetti
and even a cook. Soon a great circle of truck drivers gathered round the fire. We were the main attraction, apart
from the aroma of the stew.

Lunch and conversation lasted until late in the afternoon. There was a cheerful atmosphere despite the
wretched isangos, insects that burrow under the skin and
cause intolerable itching. At six the road was reopened
and we continued on to Nescuilla, where we slept.

Friday the 23rd brought a rainy dawn, so we were
unable to move for the morning. The Cambalaches, quite

proud of their pupils, introduced us to the commander of the local garrison, who then invited us to lunch.

As we talked at the lunch table some people came looking for the "Argentine doctors," because a sixteen-year-old lad had fallen from a truck and hurt his face. He was bleeding from the mouth, and although it looked bad, it turned out not to be very serious. Exchanging a look, Fúser and I impressed upon them the need to take the lad to the hospital in Pucallpa for an X-ray to check on internal injury. We obtained a safe conduct to go through all the checkpoints, no matter what the condition of the roads. We soon left, but hadn't gone more than five miles when we came across a long queue of trucks halted by the authorities because of the dreadful road conditions. We waved our pass, but as the truck maneuvered up the convoy, one of the drivers we knew asked us to examine one of his assistants, who was unwell. We found him to be developing pneumonia. After managing to get some vials of penicillin from the local health station, we injected him with an initial dose. We continued our journey—and what a journey!

The rain-soaked road was as slippery as soap. Our truck skidded along, threatening to send us to the bottom of a ravine or to crash into the dense forest of pine and capirona or the graceful groves of yagrumas, ceibonas and tingurúes. We were buffeted by sudden squalls. Ten times or more we got stuck in the mud and had to get out and push. In the end we had as much fun as cannibals devouring a fat missionary.

We reached Pucallpa as night fell. We took the lad to the hospital and, as we were covered in mud up to our eyeballs, the Cambalaches took us home for a wash and change of clothes. We stayed for supper. Afterward we began our farewell toasts. As the evening and drinking progressed we turned melancholic. We began to get nostalgic, swore eternal friendship and were profuse in our thanks. All we needed was a guitar and we would have been weeping tangos.

On the night of the 24th, after a delicious dinner at the Cambalaches' and taking a few souvenir photos, we set out to see the town. It is typical of the area: sprawling wooden houses, muddy streets and pavements full of obstructions.

All the timber of the Loreto region converges on the port of Pucallpa. In this city new wealth rubs shoulders with age-old poverty. The bars and brothels do a roaring trade with the hundreds of workers from the logging industry, who haul mahogany, cedar, shiringa, copal and precious rubber sap out of the depths of the forest. Then there are the river men, who ply the Ucayali and after months in the balatá or gutta-percha forests, with no other company but their machetes and mosquitoes, come here to be relieved of their hard-earned money by bar owners and brothel sirens.

This afternoon we talked to the captain of this launch, *La Cenepa*, and arranged to travel with him. As we awaited departure we swam in the Ucayali. Near us a dolphin was leaping about. The Chuncho Indians believe that the creature is a demon that kidnaps and copulates with women who bathe in the river. They also say that the female dolphin has genitals and breasts similar to those of a woman and that fishermen copulate with it. At the moment of ejaculation, however, a man must either kill the dolphin or be tied to her for ever.

We visited the regional hospital. We saw some terrible diseases, although we were also fascinated by the world of tropical medicine, with so many things to investigate and discover.

Today is the 25th, and we have been sailing for some time. *La Cenepa* is a two-deck launch that tows a smaller boat hauling a jumble of timber, swine and third-class passengers.

On the lower deck is the machine room, a wood store and the galley. On the upper are the bridge, the cabins and a covered deck that serves as dining room, recreation room, casino and nursery.

The passengers are timber merchants, rubber planters, a few adventurers and two or three tourists. Among the fair sex reigns a young girl who is quite pretty and knows it. All the ship's Don Juans sniff around her, much to the horror of two nuns and three or four scandalized old ladies whose self-esteem, I think, is slightly wounded.

Among the passengers a typical young Lima office employee stands out for his candor. He's on holiday and, like hundreds of Argentines we've known, has never before set foot outside the concrete jungle. The trip from Lima has been a constant source of suffering and misfortune comparable only to Ulysses' Odyssey. His visible fear has made him a target of the taunts of a number of other passengers, but Fúser is his defender. As ever, his timely and barbed ripostes, which are also profound and caustic, have managed to make the other passengers leave the poor office boy in peace.

The Amazon River, 26 May 1952
As we travel down the river it begins to look more and more like the Paraná. This resemblance stirs up memories of my childhood in Villa Constitución and of holidays in the city of Paraná, the capital of the province of Entre Ríos, the setting of my first dances and schoolboy love affairs.

The river gets wider as it proceeds north. Along the way are dotted a series of ports that have no connection to the outside world other than this waterway. We've sailed past islands of seemingly impenetrable forest from which timber and rubber are extracted and taken by raft to Pucallpa.

We spent the day reading and playing cards. The office boy has brought with him an array of cards and dice. His theatrical poses remind me of Luis Sandrini's[2] caricature of a hardened cardsharp.

At the request of some of the passengers we played twenty-one. Fúser won sixty soles and I twenty. That afternoon we played again. I lost thirty but as Pelao broke even we ended up winning overall.

The Amazon, 27 May 1952

Each day our progress is slower. The river is very low and it takes great skill to avoid running aground. Sometimes a dinghy has to be sent ahead to check the depth of the channel. Once the route has been determined, we slip slowly onward between picturesque islands dense with vegetation.

Parading before us is a vast sample of flora—the roda tree, used to make perfume; the haucapí, impenetrable to insects, and thus ideal for the construction of houses; the remo caspi, a very hard wood, along with the lagarto caspi, used in boat-building and for beams; and the pona palmers, which the Chama Indians use to make their bows.

This information came from an elderly shopkeeper from Iquitos, who knew as much about the region's flora as any botany professor. In response to our questions he went on to point out a huge range of medicinal plants, some of which, he says, appear to have tremendous therapeutic properties. Mallow and lancetilla, for example, are used in infusions for insomnia; verbena for fever; ñuño picanilla is a vigorous purgative; the cisa rose is used for bronchitis; chuchuhuasa for asthma (we must get some for Fúser); cotahua latex is used in the forest to stanch wounds; the chirisango to knit fractures; and so on. He

---

[2] Luis Sandrini (1905–74), a popular Argentine comic film and theater actor.

also showed us a creeper, the capironilla, used to cure insect bites.

Night overtook us as we listened and took notes. The marvelous spectacle of the setting sun stole my attention away. It bled into the river like a wounded bird and stained the water crimson. But my quiet contemplation was rudely interrupted by an invasion of huge blood-sucking mosquitoes. We slept very badly.

The Amazon, 29–30 May 1952

Life on board is unchanging. The dark young beauty is still raising havoc among the ugly sex with her frequent, daring changes of attire, her cheek and her fluttering lashes. Fúser and I are no exception to the rule. I myself am particularly susceptible to tropical beauty. And she is fascinated by our stories of what we have seen and the wonders still to come. She has made up her mind to take to the road herself. Consequently, both Fúser and I, without stepping on each other's toes, attempt to instruct her. Fees, of course, are to be paid in advance and in kind.

The river and its banks grow more beautiful every day. Now, at seven in the evening, after a fiery sunset, the landscape has taken on a grayish tinge, darkening toward the trees. Gradually the first stars come out. Under the spell of all this beauty, my thoughts turn homewards. I wholeheartedly hope that my family is as happy and content as I am now.

The Amazon, 30–31 May 1952

Our pace of life has not altered. The little miss flirts both with good conversationalists like ourselves and with good payers like the man who oversees the gaming table. The office boy is permanently terrified of allegedly poisonous spiders and a backwoods millionaire devastates his audience with his wealth.

The dinghy serves as a guide for our vessel, but also for catching fish to supplement our meals. Fúser and I always go out to throw the net. This afternoon, in addition to our usual fish, we caught a small alligator.

I daydream the evenings away, under the spell of the landscape. With the night, we enter into unequal combat with the hordes of mosquitoes.

Iquitos, 1 June 1952

We moored in this Amazon port after an excruciating night, besieged by millions of mosquitoes. This city of 50,000 knew times of splendor when rubber was needed for the war. Now that its most flourishing industry has dwindled, the city and its inhabitants struggle on in semi-poverty, and an undeserved one at that, since the climate, the fertile soil and much else demonstrate the myriad opportunities there are for turning the place into one of the richest parts of the country. To make this happen, of course, the government would have to furnish direction and financial backing.

As soon as we disembarked—Fúser in the throes of a bad asthma attack—we began to look for lodgings. Fortunately we were armed with a letter from Maestro Pesce. Within the hour we were installed in a room at the Centre for the Prevention of Yellow Fever and had put in an appearance at the general hospital, where we would have our meals. After giving Ernesto an adrenalin shot, I went to the post office in search of letters. Not a single one! I gave vent to a fit of rage—I could easily have hit someone. I made the employee go through all the letters again and had a word with the postmaster. But, in the end, I had to accept reality: there were no letters.

I returned to our lodgings. I wanted to send a cable, but Fúser made me see that this might worry my family more and wouldn't actually solve anything. His reasoning gradually calmed my frustration and upset. I tore up a letter of rebuke I was then engaged in writing and began a more rational version. But I am concerned, because it may mean that they've had no letters from me either and will be scared that something has befallen me.

At lunchtime we went to the hospital. It's part of the chain run by the Interamerican Service (SICA). The building has three wings. One is for maternity and women, the second is for men and first aid, and the third for clinical labs, a pharmacy and a staff canteen.

Healthcare is free, but patients have to pay for tests, medicine, X-rays, etc. The Tingo María and Pucallpa hospitals were similar. What's sad is that all the costs are borne by the Peruvian state. In other words, SICA serves only to show Peruvians that they are unable to run things for themselves without the tutelage of Uncle Sam.

During lunch we met a doctor who was most enthusiastic about our journey—not a common thing in our profession. He showed us round the hospital, and we saw some cases of rare illnesses. What made the greatest impression on us was a fourteen-year-old lad with terminal pemphigo. His skin was covered in blisters, which ruptured and would fall off, leaving the muscle without protection. It looks like a burn. The patient feels no pain, but withers and dies. Awful!

Iquitos, 2–5 June 1952

The last few days have been quite boring. I have been in the leprosy section, working on a series of bacilloscopes. I made several fruitless trips to the post office and, as Fúser was under the weather with his asthma and I didn't feel like doing much of anything at all, we stayed put and saw very little of Iquitos.

En route to the San Pablo leprosarium

On board El Cisne, *sailing down the Amazon, 6 June 1952*

After a number of delays and postponements we finally set sail for San Pablo. We are traveling in a small motor launch called *El Cisne*, which would be perfect for four but, of course, is carrying sixteen.

Strangely enough, the second-in-command is the brother of a nurse at the Guía Hospital, so we have been very well looked after. At this very instant I am witnessing a curious duel between the sun, which has not yet disappeared, and the moon, which is trying to outshine and eclipse it. The spectacle is so beautiful that I long for Joshua's power to stay the stars and enjoy all the longer what I see before me. I am not Joshua, so I'll try to console myself with a young schoolteacher who is angelically beautiful. (I seem to be waxing biblical today.)

The Amazon, 7 June 1952

The moon was very beautiful last night. We could even make out different species of trees at the water's edge. Unfortunately the schoolteacher left the boat at the next port, wasting my lunar inspiration.

At dawn, the calm night turned into a torrential downpour. It seemed to rain more inside our tiny cabin than out. Huddled up against the rain, the first officer told us his life story—and it was straight out of Gorky. This journey keeps proving that life contains things beyond our wildest imaginings.

Our storyteller, called Casanova, comes from a middle-class family. His mother, a widow but with some means, looked down on his taste for music and bohemian living, and his desire to wander the rivers of the Amazon. Out of love and respect for her, he gave in and studied accountancy. He worked for the same bank as his father and rose to become manager of one of the largest branches.

Some ten years ago his mother died and that same day, he said—and I quote his very words—"I came back from the cemetery and took off my tie for ever. In my shirt-sleeves, with my guitar slung over my shoulder, I went straight to the office of the managing director to hand in my resignation. He was so surprised he couldn't even open his mouth."

Then he sold off his furniture, clothes and whatever else he could and used the money to buy a share of *El Cisne*. Since then he has plied the Ucayali, Marañón, Amazon and Negro Rivers. Depending on the season he travels deep into Brazil, Colombia or Ecuador, but has never again set foot in Lima. He is quite certainly a happy man, because he has made his dream come true. Perhaps a less determined man would have stayed put, passively and unhappily sighing over an unfulfilled dream.

That morning we stopped at one of the many hamlets that dot the river bank and islands. But this one was different. One of the inhabitants was quite skillful and hard-working and had managed to graft oranges and lemons onto a citrus trunk unaffected by the constant flooding that rots ordinary citrus trees. Avarice, unfortunately, is what drives him and, as he alone has this graft, he sells his fruit very dear. Furthermore, he lives in fear of someone stealing a plant and setting up in competition. Fúser was quite sarcastic and told him in no uncertain terms that his selfish attitude blighted the admiration we felt at his hard work and intelligence.

After this conversation and to make our feelings even clearer, Fúser and I delved into the thicket in search of wild fruit, avocado and star apples. When we got back to the boat Casanova presented us with half a sackful of oranges and lemons, which the guy had sent as a gift to Fúser.

We journeyed on. All that afternoon and evening we listened to Casanova playing his guitar and singing Peruvian songs, especially waltzes. I copied out one of them— "Heart, Soul and Life"—to learn myself and have as a reminder of these marvelous times and these extraordinary men.

Science in the jungle

The leprosarium of San Pablo, 18 June 1952

The rain is torrential. A thick gray veil hides the shapes of the trees and I am overcome by sadness.

I torture myself looking for explanations of why I've had no letters from home. Neither the strength of the downpour nor the imposing sight of the river can distract me, so I've turned to writing to alleviate my tension. I will take this chance to recap events since our arrival.

It was about three in the morning on Sunday the 8th and Dr. Bresciani, the director, hearing that the "Argentine scientists" had arrived, got up to greet us. He invited us into his home until a room could be made ready for us. The moonlit night gave us a good view of the buildings and layout of the colony.

It is composed of several wooden buildings, on stilts, scattered round the clearing. Apart from the dining hall, the buildings are one story tall and long, with a row of rooms one after the other. These buildings are connected by plank walkways about three feet off the ground, which enable the inhabitants to move around without getting muddy, as the rainfall is heavy and frequent, particularly during the season they refer to as winter, which actually falls in the months of spring and summer.

As we spoke with the director and contemplated the small town, we were informed that our room was ready. We went along, accompanied by an immense cloud of mosquitoes, welcoming us in their nasty way.

We slept like logs until eleven the next morning. The director invited us to lunch. Conversation revolved around Dr. Pesce and the help he gives them from Lima, especially scientific support, as little can be done materially.

In the afternoon we were invited to play soccer. You have to go by boat to the pitch, which is in a clearing about a mile upstream. The trip was made in an outboard motor boat.

I was daft with happiness—playing soccer in the middle of the jungle—but as ever my thoughts turned to how wonderful it would be if only Grego and Maso were here too. During the game I paid more attention to my surroundings than to the ball, so I played rather badly. Afterward we went and swam in a small river inlet. The temperature of the water was just right. Who knows how long we would have lazed there, if the inevitable horde of mosquitoes hadn't appeared on the scene. We ran toward the main canteen, waving our arms like windmills to drive away the wretched insects. Several of our fellow sportsmen were waiting for us there and bought us some beers.

On the 9th we visited the asylum. The daily round is as follows: the doctors, the dentist and the auxiliaries get changed in a small room on a raft moored to the colony's landing stage. Inside there are two changing rooms, separated by a corridor with showers.

In the first room they completely disrobe and in the other they don the garments for the sick quarters. When we were all loaded up, a motor boat took us half a mile downriver to the sanatorium.

My first impression of the hospital was that we'd just arrived at another normal riverside village. The houses are built of pona wood, randomly laid out, shops open to passersby; canoes and motor boats come and go, laden with bunches of bananas, papaya, fresh or salt fish.

But soon our attention was directed to a painful sight. The majority of the men and women had numerous lesions and mutilations. Both their feet and their hands revealed the indelible marks of the evil that afflicts them, as well as loss of phalanxes or whole digits.

The percentage of patients affected by these mutilations was so high that at the earliest opportunity I remarked on this to the doctor accompanying us. He confirmed my first impression, telling me that other leprologists, such as Souza Lima and Fernández, have made the same observation without any explanation for the phenomenon having yet been discovered.

We arrived at the offices, as the doctor's and dentist's surgeries are called here. They are all in the same building, raised on wooden stilts. There is a general surgery for related diseases and another for the director, where specialist consultations and minor operations may also be carried out. There is also a treatment room and, finally, a large area containing the waiting room, the dentist's surgery and the dispensary.

After observing several interesting cases and seeing how the director was gathering data for a paper on "Nervous Syndromes in Leprosy," where the remote-control guidance of Dr. Pesce was clearly evident, we took a stroll around the sanatorium.

The older buildings, made of pona wood, a type of palm quite common in these parts, are huge and poorly built. The most recent buildings, on the other hand, are made of cedar and much better.

All the patients live as families, with their wives and children. It's extremely hard to separate parents from their children. All the patients come from communities along the banks of the rivers Ucayali and Yaraví, where leprosy is endemic. Therefore, used to seeing the afflicted around them, people here find it normal to be together and absurd that anyone should want to separate them from their children.

All the same, the light of understanding is gradually straightening out their equivocal ideas, and already many of the children of the sick are in a healthy zone, in a prevention center, under observation to check whether or not they are carrying the disease. When they reach working age they are usually employed by the hospital as health workers.

On this visit we also saw several of the shops run by the sick. These vary from a fishing-tackle shop to a bar with a fridge for cold drinks. Others have cleared part of the jungle to grow tomatoes, yuccas, bananas and other crops. Some of them have done so well that they have purchased their own motor boats.

This independent way of life—so different from what we knew to be the case in Argentina—instead of propelling the patients into flight, ties them closer to the sanatorium and the plot of land they own, which has now become their real home.

We returned to the changing raft, put our shorts on and dived into the river! We swam for an hour and then went for lunch. That afternoon we were introduced to the nuns who work in the laboratory and the children's shelter. Later we went fishing with one of the doctors. We caught four or five catfish. We threw a net several times, but had less luck than with hooks; in fact, we didn't catch anything else. We barbecued the fish for supper that night.

Tuesday the 10th we spent the whole morning working at the leper colony. The afternoon was spent playing soccer. While playing I got scratched on the leg and bled a bit. Thinking nothing of it, after the game I dived head-first into the river behind Fúser.

I had hardly surfaced when I felt something sticky on my leg and then quite a sharp pain, like a hypodermic needle. I stood up and lifted my leg exclaiming, "Ernesto, what's wrong with my leg?" With his usual quick reaction, Fúser snatched at a piranha fish that was clinging to my calf, attracted to the blood from the wound. We got straight out of the water. Falling about with laughter, he showed me the tiny piece of skin, muscle and hair that the piranha had clamped between its triangular teeth.

On the 11th, while Ernesto was in clinical consultation with Dr. Bresciani, I remained in the lab studying bacilloscope samples. The work is carried out under makeshift conditions. They don't even have an electric bulb for the microscope, which isn't of very good quality anyway. Therefore the observation is done under natural light and with poor-quality lenses. Visibility not being good, the margin of error is great.

We told the director about all the difficulties we had encountered. He accepted our comments good-naturedly. It seems to me we are no longer scientists in inverted commas.

That afternoon we went out sightseeing. We were taken to a creek on one of the islands. When the river is at high water, the islands' lagoons and ponds become part of the Amazon. At its mouth the creek is as wide as any regular river in Argentina, but it soon gets narrow and branches out into the forest.

Our silent voyage amid thousands of trees that shut out the sky was a stunning experience. We encountered myriad birds of every conceivable hue and size: parrots, white and red herons, even a species of kingfisher with incredibly beautiful plumage. We also spied chameleons, boas, monkeys—basically everything one imagines seeing in boyhood dreams of adventure.

Just where the lagoons flow into the river the big fish wait in ambush for the minnows, which fatten up in the ponds when the water is low, so it is a real paradise for fishermen. We weren't equipped for fishing, but there were a couple of lines with hooks in the boat, though no bait. Fúser skewered a chunk of banana on one of the hooks and spent twenty minutes trying to attract a fish. The doctor and I began to tease him, saying we had never met a vegetarian fish and that banana was good bait if you wanted to catch monkeys. Fúser just laughed at our bad jokes, never taking his eyes off the line. Suddenly he tugged at it and out came a large cunchi.

That shut us up! We immediately chopped the fish up into bait and the three of us went into action. Soon we had a catch of eight or nine fish, including a ten-pound zúngaro. The doctor caught that one, and he was very proud of this deed because, according to the experts, it's a hard fish to catch, especially on a hook.

Radiantly happy, we returned to the sanatorium with our catch, which the doctor promised to turn into ceviche[1] As we said goodbye to him, Fúser, sardonic and to the point as ever, said, "Banana's lousy bait, eh?"

What else could the doctor and I do but laugh heartily.

Thursday the 12th I worked all morning in the lab. Pelao went on morning rounds with the doctor. For lunch we ate his famous ceviche and in the afternoon went to play soccer. I'll never tire of repeating how wonderful that short journey is, with the boat crammed full of young people off to play sport after completing their day's work.

You pull into a small bay with grassy banks graced by beautiful breadfruit trees. This is surely one of the loveliest trees I have ever set eyes on. Something like a chestnut, but broader and with leaves of a brighter green.

But this is merely an introduction to the strangest and most picturesque pitch ever imagined by a globetrotting sportsman like me! In the heart of the Amazon forest,

[1] Ceviche: a typical Peruvian dish consisting of raw fish marinated in lemon with onion and chilies.

enclosed by thickets of palm and silk-cotton trees, creepers, lianas and ornamental plants all entwined together, it's an incomparable place.

The pitch is short and wide, just like the one in the National Stadium in Córdoba, where Ernesto, Tomás, Gregorio and I have played so often. It made me think how fantastic it would be to have the three Granados in midfield, with Fúser in goal. But then the thought of the absence of news from home dampened my happiness somewhat. When we got back from the match I radioed Iquitos to see if there were any letters for us. Not one.

That night the director invited us to eat ceviche. We stuffed ourselves! When I go back to Argentina I'm going to try making it with kingfish. Just as we were off to bed, the dentist turned up and invited us to a party at his place.

When we arrived it was in full swing. A "big band," made up of two guitars and a saxophone, was murdering a Peruvian waltz. Our arrival set off a tremendous round of applause, toasts and shouted welcomes.

People were drinking beer, pisco, sweet wine and chicken soup, in no particular order and huge measures. But Fúser and I were being careful what we drank. We danced to everything: waltzes, marineras, Colombian porros and Brazilian choros, but mostly mambos and tangos, the mambo being all the rage just now and the tangos in our honor.

Friday the 13th it rained all morning, so we didn't go to the hospital. We went fishing instead, although we were told that the rain churns up the water and mud, making more food available, so the fish don't bite. And they didn't. But we met a Yagua Indian who was spear-fishing. We followed to watch how he did it. He was using thin wooden spears with points fashioned from hard wood or carved bone. The handle of the spear is tied to a piece of balsa wood—dyed white, red or blue—by a length of string about ten feet long. He cruises the creeks that flow into the river in his canoe and at the right moment, when a fish is within reach, he hurls his spear. If he hits his target he doesn't wait, but continues upstream, and the fish swims on with the harpoon stuck in its body.

As the Indian pursued his single-minded hunt for fish, we hoisted up the motor and rowed the boat so as not to break the silence. Imperturbable, despite knowing he was being watched, he continued throwing his darts. If he missed his target, he lifted the harpoon up with his paddle and went on his way without taking his eyes off the water. He tried again, and if successful left the fish flapping in the water.

In less than an hour he harpooned at least nine fish. Then he made the return journey, looking for the colored buoys among the roots and submerged branches. He collected a saltón fish here, a maparache there, the odd paiche. Sometimes the harpoon came up empty, for the fish, although wounded, had managed to escape.

Marveling at the skill of the fisherman, we returned to our residence. We were told that a party was being prepared in Ernesto's honor: tomorrow he'll be twenty-four.

An unusual birthday

On the morning of Saturday the 14th we worked at the sanatorium. At around eleven we went round visiting some of the vegetable gardens, and played soccer with a group of young patients. Afterward we talked to them about some of the Argentine soccer stars, who are as popular here as they are at home, and of course the usual subject came up: the exodus of many of our star players to Colombia.

Our conversation was so animated that the boat nearly left without us. On board, the director, in open admiration, said to us, "You two are as familiar with Joyce and García Lorca as you are with leprologists like Souza Lima and Darmendra, or with soccer players like Pedernera, Di Stefano and Labruna. You are men of science, yet love to play sport with youngsters, but what I like best of all about you is that you couldn't give a fig for what others think."

Pelao and I winked at each other and—as the saying goes—blushed like virgins.

That evening we went to a birthday dinner given by the director's wife for Fúser. Afterward we went to the canteen for the party in his honor. On the way there he said, "Look, Mial, I'm only going to dance to tangos, but what with the way these people play sometimes and my rotten ear, I can't make out what the tune is, so, when it's a tango, give me a kick under the table."

We arrived, but to our surprise the place was empty. We sat down. A few seconds later there was banging at the door and the band, lying in wait for us, burst in. They struck up "Happy Birthday," and ten or twelve young people, nurses and cleaning girls, crowded round us. Each one gave Fúser twenty-four tugs on the ear, while some of the bolder ones gave him a kiss or two. The ice was broken. More revelers arrived, and soon a tango was played. I kicked Fúser, and off he went with a pretty Indian girl to the two–four time.

People started toasting, and the pisco was soon flowing like water. Around midnight the director made a speech, complimenting the birthday boy. Ernesto replied briefly, and as usual was both precise and profound. He praised the investigative spirit and work of this hospital enclave here in the heart of the jungle, the hospitality and affection given to two outsiders they'd known nothing about and to whom they'd nonetheless opened their doors and their hearts. He was much applauded.

Just as it seemed the party was over, another was just getting under way in the residential quarters. We launched out to conquer this last redoubt, each of us with a bottle of pisco or cane brandy in hand, the musicians leading the way.

When we were seen coming, the others closed the door and turned the lights out. The band struck up a waltz about happiness and long life, the lights came on again, the door was thrown open and the merrymaking continued. Almost immediately the party spread out until there were so many people dancing that the house, up on its wooden stilts, began to shake. It looked like one of those cartoon houses that jig up and down in time to the music.

Fúser, of course, was the favorite and several girls were competing to dance with him. There was one he had his eye on. We followed our pre-arranged plan. Whenever a tango was played I gave him a kick, and everything was going smoothly, but then something happened to upset our plan. The band, after an interval, began to play a Brazilian melody that had been a favorite of Ernesto's girlfriend Chichina. Hearing it, I said to him, "Do you remember?" and I accidentally touched his foot.

Thinking I was signaling a tango, he shot off onto the dance floor with the Indian girl who had been sitting in a corner gazing at him. Before I could react, Pelao was dancing a slow tango pace in the middle of the hubbub of the other couples, who were swinging to a fast Brazilian choro. Realizing that all was not well he came over to the table where, doubled up with laughter, I tried sign language—laughing too hard to speak—to show him that the others were dancing much faster. He didn't get the message and so continued his stately 1,2,3,4, and turn, 1,2,3,4, and turn. We didn't get to bed till dawn, sweaty, tired and happy. Three hours later we were up again to pay a visit to a tribe of Yagua Indians.

During the following ten or twelve hours we had an unforgettable experience. The hospital director, who adores all kinds of adventures, had arranged with one of the nurses—son of the chief of a small Indian tribe nearby—to take us on a monkey hunt.

We went about a mile and a half upriver by boat. We left one group fishing while we headed inland with Roger, the doctor, and Tomás, the nurse.

The forest, no longer virgin but still beautiful, stretched away ahead of us. The huge trees hid the sky. The lianas hung between them, linking them. The only way into the forest was by a tiny path known to the trackers.

After a few minutes' walk we came to the village. The chief was waiting for us, surrounded by his womenfolk and an indeterminate number of children. The smallest of them, with a moving display of trust, climbed straight into my arms. They were all wearing their traditional palm-fiber clothing.

The community lives in a large sort of shelter where the women cook and the children play. They have a communal dormitory, which is like a spherical oven, made of woven palm leaves, with a small entrance, hermetically sealed to keep out mosquitoes. Parents, children, brothers and sisters—all pile in together.

We set off with the chief in the direction of the departing hunters. The dense forest gradually thinned out. After half a mile or so we saw what appeared to be a cascade of clear water falling from the sky. Tomás explained that it was the effect of the light filtering through the trees, as the area had been defoliated by the passing monkeys.

Drawing closer to the illuminated area we saw that it was like a large window a few miles long and some fifty yards wide, in which the tree branches had been stripped bare. As we arrived we were told to anoint our faces and hands with a mixture of monkey grease and annatto to neutralize the mosquitoes as well as our human scent, which might alert the animals to our presence. We crouched down close to a group of women and older children. One of the hunters, down on his haunches fifty feet from us, held a blowpipe in one hand and a dart dipped in curare in the other.

There was a half-hour wait before we began to hear what sounded like puppies barking. We all ducked down. I expected the animals to appear any second but what seemed like a long, long time went by and nothing happened. We waited interminably, maybe more than three-quarters of an hour. The monkeys' howls became clearer with every passing minute.

Suddenly, just when I thought I was completely alert, I was surprised by the shadows of a pair of monkeys of more than medium size that passed shrieking above our heads. They were immediately followed by hundreds of monkeys of all sizes, male and female, many with their young clinging to them, moving noisily through the leafless area. It was hard to keep still. Fúser and I both had our eyes fixed on the hunter.

The whole troop passed us, and no one moved. Two or three minutes later another group of eight monkeys came past. Then four more. A few minutes later all one heard was the shrieking of the animals in the distance. But then a single monkey appeared, quite a big one with three others in tow. When the last of this group passed the thicket where the Indian was crouching with his blowpipe, it suddenly dropped like ripe fruit. One of the women beside us sped out and carried the animal back in her arms. We ran over to see it. It was rigid, and only the movement of its pupils showed that it was not dead but paralyzed by the poisoned dart. Taking the creature in my arms, I was surprised at how heavy it was in relation to its size.

Then came the explanations. We were told that you must be very careful only to kill the animals trailing at the back of the troop because, if the others see a killing, they change course and the hunting ground is then lost.

Gradually the other hunters turned up. Five monkeys in all were taken. Carrying one of them on a pole, we returned to the village. They proposed that we stay to eat the meat. We accepted.

While lunch was being prepared we went for a stroll. We tried our hand at the blowpipe. We also visited a little garden where the Indians were growing chilies similar to the ones in Argentina that we call "bloody hellfire."

Dr. Bresciani told us that the Indians eat a lot of this chili. Considering the information in biochemical terms, we concluded this excessive consumption must be due to it being a rich source of vitamin C.

As we returned we smelt the roast. The chief invited us to a gourd full of mazato, an alcoholic drink produced by fermenting cassava. So involved were we in trying to make ourselves understood to the Indian chief and the other hunters that we didn't see that the director and Tomás had slipped away.

Soon we were called to eat. We sat down in the hut in front of huge plantain leaves for plates. We were served boiled cassava and plantain. While we were eating, Roger and Tomás appeared with a platter containing a roast monkey that looked like a newborn baby.

Fúser and I looked at each other. Obviously, the joke was on us. We plucked up our courage and asked to be served straight away as we were starving.

At the very first bite I felt my tongue burning. I can't even say I know what monkey meat tastes like—all I felt was the burning of the chili.

With such spicy food, we had to have several more drinks of mazato. This gave my friends another good chance to laugh. After I had drunk four or five gourdfuls I was asked whether I liked it.

"Sure," I said. "Can't you tell?" And I had another swig.

"Do you want to come and see how it's made?"

I said yes and followed them to a place not far away. The spectacle before my eyes, if not quite Dante's inferno, was certainly horrifying. There were five or six women sitting round a shallow bowl, smoking and chatting. Some toothless, others with beautiful teeth, they were all chewing lumps of cassava, which they then spat into the bowl.

As we surveyed the scene Tomás said, "There's your delicious mazato."

I felt a sudden heave in my stomach. All this combined—the human semblance of the roast monkey, the acrid smell of the grease we'd been smeared with, and now, to crown it all, the Indian women spitting into the bowl—proved stronger than my nervous system. I tore into the undergrowth to vomit up everything I had eaten and drunk.

Shortly afterward, on my feet again, we returned to the landing stage where we had left the other group fishing. They'd been anxious about our delay. We returned to the colony and stayed up into the small hours turning over the details of the hunt.

Yesterday, Tuesday the 17th, Pelao fulfilled another of his dreams: to swim across the Amazon. Despite many warnings about the danger—alligators and piranhas, which as we now know are quick to appear on the scene at the slightest trace of blood—he was insistent. I, of course, wasted no time in trying to dissuade him. I merely made him promise that if he was gashed by one of the hundreds of branches or logs dragged along by the current, he would immediately climb back on board the boat.

We set out at about two in the afternoon. The river at that point is almost a mile wide, but Ernesto swam with the current and then, about midway, he turned on his back and drifted for ten minutes. He kept swimming and came out on the other side about three miles downstream from the colony.

Panting but happy, he climbed into the boat. We returned with quite a crowd—one of the doctors, Roger, the director's brother-in-law and some other young people who were accompanying me in the boat and couldn't hide their admiration of Fúser's courage.

That night we celebrated his feat. The organizer of the party was someone from administration, a homosexual with delusions of grandeur. He's always going on about parties and soirées at his place, horse rides with famous doctors, artists and government leaders. Quite clearly all figments of his imagination.

Using the fact that he had organized the affair, he made a long speech, by turns boastful and coarse, and was quite oblivious to the many attempts to interrupt him. He said that all present, apart from the director and us, were poor ignorant devils with no social graces who profited from the presence of educated people in the colony to better themselves. At last he wound up and the obligatory toasts were made. I hardly touched a glass, since my stomach was still wobbly from Sunday's excursion. We soon headed for bed.

So, there's a summary of our first ten days at the San Pablo leprosarium. As I said at the beginning of these notes, torrential rain began again today, so we spent all morning looking into a new plan—traveling to Leticia by raft. We intend to build it from a piece of a huge raft used to transport cattle here.

Alfaro and Chávez, two colony employees, are helping us refashion the craft. The raft is made of twelve logs of bolsa (a low-density wood native to this area, which floats well), secured by lianas. It is three yards wide by seven long. There's a small covered dwelling of palm leaves in the center, called a tambo in the local rafters' slang. It is looking good. We're pleased as punch when we think of our Amazon journey, and all through our own efforts.

San Pablo leprosarium, 19 June 1952

As there are no rounds on Thursday, a group of us went fishing. We took tackle, including a net, but also a little money to "catch" some fruit.

Overall we caught twenty huge fish, including three maparates and gaminotes. These are enormous fish weighing more than twelve pounds each. We also caught some gigantic sardines and a type of dorado, which in these parts is called a golden sardine.

We stopped at several farms and bought and ate about a dozen papaya.

Toward midday we chanced upon an enormous zúngaro idling near the surface. Tomás, the nurse, who under a thin layer of civilization hides pure Yagua Indian blood, grabbed a harpoon, cut the motor and rowed toward the fish. He immediately reminded me of the Indian we had seen a few days earlier. If it wasn't for his clothes he would have been the spitting image of the other one.

He inched to within about fifteen feet of the fish and, as it sped off, he hurled the harpoon with such marksmanship that it struck the fish amidships. Unfortunately, as the harpoon was buoyless, the big creature hid itself among the rushes at the river bank.

Just seconds later the heavens opened and a strong wind began to whip up waves as though we were at sea.

Roger, who was a little peeved at Pelao's feat of swimming the river, wanted to cross to the other bank to show off his courage, but when the boat began to spin around and fill with water he took fright and returned to the shore. He is such a show-off that we had to tease him, for the tremendous fright on his face invited laughter as well as sympathy.

When the wind let up we crossed the river and disembarked. We barbecued the fish and spent the rest of the day watching the rain and recalling the time spent in San Pablo.

An unforgettable send-off

On board the Mambo-Tango *raft, 20 June 1952*

L ast night we were shown such affection by the patients, surely one of the sweetest memories of my life. It happened as follows: round about seven in the evening we were called to the jetty. There, under a persistent drizzle, was one of the patients' boats, completely full of men, women and children. As we arrived they shouted several Hurrahs! and then sang us some songs. Most of the staff had also gathered there. The colony band, led by the saxophone player, regaled us with one tune after another.

The time flew and night fell. Three of the patients made speeches. Simply, almost shyly, they told us of their admiration for our voyage and their appreciation of the way we had treated them.

As the third one concluded, Fúser gave me a gentle shove and I prepared to reply. With a lump in my throat I could hardly start. I was so moved that I did not express myself very well initially, but in the end it sounded all right.

Several songs followed. Then another patient, the teacher, spoke briefly but with great feeling, on behalf of all the patients and staff. As the applause died away they sang a farewell song and the boat slipped silently and slowly away. It was the most moving part of the evening: that white boat gently departing into the rainy night while their raised voices still reached our ears. More like a dream than reality. But it was a reality of kindness and caring, of a common love of humanity that binds us all.

This morning we visited the colony for the last time. The children, now knowing we don't fear contagion, came to say goodbye, inviting us to share their pineapple rings and custard apples. They even gave us two pineapples for the journey.

The older people gave us advice and told us to beware of logjams piling up in the river—they entwine with liana and are dragged by the current. Apparently, if they collide with the raft they could easily break it up.

We returned to the hospital and then to the non-infected area. As we bade our farewells and put the finishing touches to the raft they painted a sign that said on one side MAMBO and on the other TANGO. So our craft is named *Mambo-Tango*.

Every single person wanted to give us some food—consequently we have provisions for a month instead of a couple of days. We have butter, sausages, tinned meat, flour, lentils, chickpeas and much more. Also a lantern, kerosene, a mosquito net, fresh eggs, papaya, a bunch of bananas and even two live chickens.

The display of so much affection overwhelmed us and we were going round and round until Fúser, decisive as ever said, "Come on, Mial, take a photo and we're off."

So we took several pictures and embarked. The director and Chávez, our boatbuilder, helped us to maneuver it into midstream. Roger and Montoya followed in the motor boat to bring them back.

Once in midstream, we tried out the beam-end oar, which serves as a rudder, to see if we could handle the craft. Satisfied that we could, they returned to the other boat.

We asked them to take a photo of the two of us in the

middle of the river. As they returned the camera they embraced us in turn, balancing one foot on the raft, the other in the boat.

We were soon passing the asylum, where many people waved farewell. Finally we were out in the middle of the Amazon, under our own steam.

We were so excited we couldn't keep still. We set ourselves to racing a log that had just overtaken us. We rowed for half an hour until we had left it several hundred yards behind.

Tired and more relaxed, we sat in the shadow of the shelter and ate to distract ourselves: papaya, cheese, sausage, bread—in no particular order. Later we killed one of the chickens, plucked and hung it in the shade to keep it fresh.

As I write, Fúser has been hanging the mosquito net and lighting the lantern. With nightfall we need to be visible as we will soon be passing Chimbote, the last Peruvian garrison, and we don't want them mistaking us for smugglers and pumping us full of lead.

That's enough diary for now, I must help Pelao row as the raft has pulled over to the left and Chimbote is on the other side.

Mambo-Tango *raft, the Amazon, 21 June 1952*

Last night, despite our strenuous rowing, we could hardly shift the raft toward midstream. As the inevitable mosquitoes turned up we did ten-minute turns each. Suddenly the lights of Chimbote appeared. We tried to steer the raft toward the wharf, but it was impossible. Minutes later the lights had disappeared. And the garrison never even knew.

Upset at having swept by so helplessly, we tried to steer the raft toward the side in readiness for the next frontier post. Our attempts were unsuccessful, so we gave up and crept under the mosquito net to sleep.

We woke to find ourselves rammed against a logjam on the right-hand bank. Using the oars we pushed the raft into the current again and set to preparing breakfast. It was about eight o'clock. At the back of our shelter we had a patch of moist soil on which we built a fire. As it turned to embers we drank maté and cast the line that the patients had given us. As we were finishing the maté I saw that the twine holding the line to the raft was twitching, so I began to haul it in. At first it didn't feel very strong, but I soon had to shout for Pelao, who was at the other end chopping up the chicken.

After a twenty-minute struggle we hauled the fish out. It was a huge saltón that weighed twenty-five pounds. We gutted it and put it in the shade so that it wouldn't go bad. An hour later we spied a house and, despite our store of victuals, seeing a cassava patch made us think how good some barbecued cassava would be. The current had brought us toward the shore, so the approach was easy.

As we drew up, Fúser, the stronger of us, tried to hold the raft still while I attempted to jump off. But just then the two logs serving as a landing stage opened up like a compass and there I was, stuck, my feet on one log and my hands on the other. I made my way crab-wise to the point where the logs met, while Fúser tried to use the oars to steady the raft. Finally he threw me our liana mooring rope, and I was able to hitch it to a post.

Having solved that little difficulty, I now faced another: how to make myself understood to the Indian woman whose cassava it was. After several frustrating attempts I opted for a practical way out. I filled a basket with several cassavas worth about two soles and, being quite Peruvianized by now, I offered her thirty cents. She refused. I upped it to half a sol. Reading her silence as assent, I shouldered the basket. I emptied and returned it and we continued on.

We immediately put two cassavas to cook in the fire

and prepared the chicken. It was quite tough, so we boiled it a bit before frying, then added the giblets, rice, pasta and garlic to the broth. That soup would have raised the dead!

After the soup we just kept going. For hors d'oeuvres before lunch we ate one of the huge pineapples. We tucked in, and as the juice ran down our sparse beards I couldn't resist saying to Fúser, "It's true then what they say about travel broadening the mind and improving one's manners. Just look at you: what a perfect example!"

When we could stop laughing we went back to the fruit and then threw the line out again, using chicken fat as bait.

No sooner had I cast the line than it was tugged right out of my hand. Thankfully it was tied to the raft, so I grabbed it again and began hauling it in, shouting for Ernesto, who was attending to the frying pan.

Some ten yards from the raft a huge saltón leaped at least three feet out of the water. By the time Pelao could come to my aid, the fish was no longer pulling and we realized that it had taken the hook with it, which itself weighed a good pound and a half, snapping the heavy-weight mason's line.

Dusk was fast approaching. The current was very strong, so we decided we'd better keep watch in one hour shifts. We were just getting ready when we suddenly realized that the raft was heading directly and swiftly for a tree that was sticking out of the river. We rowed furiously in an effort to avoid the tree and its limbs, but it still seemed that we were going to collide, which would probably damage the raft. Fúser crouched at the front edge of the raft and, as we neared one of the thickest branches, he grabbed onto and leaned against it to brake our movement. Meanwhile I wielded an oar like a lever, and our combined efforts shot the raft off past the danger.

During the commotion, and owing to some slight damage to our roof caused by the branches, the remaining chicken got loose. It jumped into the water as we ran after it. We stared at each other and for an instant we hesitated. Maybe it was the failing light, our exhaustion or the speed of the raft—I don't know—but in that instant of vacillation we lost the chicken, and indeed it had soon disappeared from view.

It is now eleven-thirty. Fúser is snoring. The raft slips placidly onward under a firmament so brimming with stars that it looks silvery. I bend to my writing, sitting by the lantern, but with one eye alert for any mysterious shadow of a logjam or a half-submerged tree trunk.

My mind turns homeward. I would give anything right now to be with my family, just to tell them how well and happy I am. I think I must take some money home to try and provide some material comforts. Of course, I could make money in Argentina, but I have to reconcile my urge to travel with my desire to help. And why shouldn't I do it this way?

The Amazon River, 22 June 1952

This morning we found ourselves already in Brazilian territory. We passed the settlements of Ramón Castilla and Leticia in the small hours, probably about 2 a.m.

While on watch we each saw some faint lights on the shore. Still, as both places are border ports, we thought they would have had searchlights or something to make them stand out; anyway, we trusted that if a raft or any other vessel did not stop, they would send a launch out to investigate.

In any case, when we saw a house we went up and asked when we would reach Leticia. We were told that it was two hours behind us and that we were in Brazil. We moored up at this house and, in our broken Portuguese, managed to negotiate an agreement by which we'd leave the raft with the man and he'd convey us back upriver in a small dugout he has made from a hollow tree. I'm already delighting in the prospect of such a novel trip.

The family invited us to eat, and we gave them the remaining pineapple and the virtually complete bunch of bananas and several bottles of kerosene, which will be useful for them. These people live in a dreadful state. They are afflicted by hookworm and pestered by the gnat-like paracana. Most of them are anemic, which makes them apathetic and listless. They are but shadows of human beings.

Leticia, 23 June 1952

Today's adventure was a real treat. For more than five hours we were paddled up the Amazon in an Indian dugout. The first hour was tough going, but after that the effort involved seemed less.

As the going was slow I was able to look around and watch crowds of little monkeys pirouetting through the trees. Around one o'clock we ate a little fish, fried plantain and a papaya. We soon continued on, the Brazilian in the stern, me amidships and Fúser in the bow. We left around nine and reached Leticia at about three in the afternoon.

Once on Colombian soil we went to the police, then to the army barracks and finally to the customs police, where we explained how we had arrived. They stamped entry permits in our passports saying that we "disembarked from a raft," with the word for raft misspelled. I will try to hang on to this passport, not because of the quaint mistake, but because I think it shows a rather original way to enter a country and will make a good souvenir.

After some negotiations we managed to get lodgings at police headquarters and a meal at the police station. We collected our gear from the port and went to our lodgings.

Our welcome so far has been rather cool, but perhaps it will "improve with age."

The town is tiny, almost entirely composed of government employees, customs police and soldiers.

To think of so much Peruvian and Colombian blood spilled for this patch of land and, worst of all, that both sides think it was worth it.

Leticia, 24 June 1952

Last night I slept like a log but kept paddling. I was delighting in the birds and their fabulous plumage, admiring the slender palm trees and the delicate colors of the butterflies. In short, I relived those unforgettable moments in my dreams.

That afternoon we went to meet the colonel in charge of the local garrison and some other officers. They are quite uncouth and had neither books nor magazines and were unable to sustain a normal conversation. As soon as we could we made good our escape.

Leticia, 25 June 1952

Today we met one of the local doctors. He's quite a broad-minded man. We had an interesting conversation with him. He's in charge of some reforms being introduced at the new hospital. He seems interested in everything. While we were with him he dealt with a series of problems from administration to bricklaying and carpentry, demonstrating his concern for all hospital matters.

In the afternoon we went to the port to try to exchange soles for Colombian pesos with a boat heading for Peru. It seems our fame goes before us. Some sailors and customs workers told us that the first officer of *El Cisne* had told them about "two scientists doing a tour of all the leprosaria in the world."

That evening one of the directors of the Independiente

Sporting Football Club paid us a visit. What salary would we require to stay and train his team? We replied that we couldn't agree a salary as we did not know how long we'd stay but that tomorrow we would go to the pitch and, depending on what we do and how well, they can pay us accordingly.

From leprologists to soccer players

Leticia, 26 June 1952

A t five this morning, with the sun already high, we
went to the soccer ground. The players have little
control over the ball, but they are tireless and very obedi-
ent. Their style of play is similar to Argentina's in the thir-
ties—the goalkeeper fixed in goal, the defense in their own
area, and the midfielders running all over the place.

We gave them some instruction in close marking. After
half an hour's practice we played a game with the defenders against the strikers, and they were amazed at the
results of the marking. A practice game is needed to show
them the link between defense and attack.

On our way back, we called in at the home of one of the
players and, for lack of anything better, we borrowed a
geography text and a history of Colombia for bedtime
reading.

Leticia, 27 June 1952

Last night one of the lieutenants in command of the garrison invited us for a few beers. The alcohol made him talkative, and he told us a few stories about the guerrilla struggle. As far as we could make out from what he said, the
government is trying to pass off as just some commotion
on the plains what is in fact a real guerrilla war, already a
decade old.

He told us an experience of his own when he was a sergeant and his garrison was attacked. The siege lasted ten

days, an intense firefight leaving ten dead and more than twenty injured. He himself took two bullets. In Bogotá they thought him dead and had even bestowed posthumous honors on him. His "heroic act" earned him promotion and it seems to have gone to his head.

This morning we had another training session with the players. They seem keen to learn. We're trying to work in some new techniques. The defense are proving reluctant to leave their area, fearing they'll expose the goalkeeper. It's easy when Fúser is in goal, because he shouts at them where to place themselves and who to mark, but with the regular goalkeeper they are less relaxed.

Afterward we went to the hospital, where we saw some malaria cases. This evening we met up with some of the players and talked about soccer and tactics until a short while ago.

Leticia, 28 June 1952

Today's Saturday. After the training session we went for a walk. We crossed the Colombian border and entered Brazil.

We happened upon the farm of a very resourceful peasant-farmer. In eight months he has transformed the plot of land given to him by the government into a proper farm, and been offered 3,000 Colombian pesos for it. He is also beginning to exploit the timber of the surrounding forest, albeit in a primitive fashion. He invited us to come back and have lunch on Sunday.

This afternoon we visited a Colombian merchant marine ship that transports paving stones. It had run aground. The ship is worth several million pesos. All that's needed to float it again is to build a gangplank and unload its cargo. Apart from the ship being left to slowly deteriorate, the government is paying—with the people's money, of course—for a crew to hang around in bars down at the docks. I remarked on this inertia on the part of the government. Never one to miss a trick, Ernesto said, "Don't you see it's a sort of show of strength by Colombia vis-à-vis Brazil and Peru?"

Perhaps he's right.

Leticia, 29 June 1952

There is a one-day knockout tournament this afternoon, so early this morning we played a practice match against a team much better than ours. Fúser refereed, and I was the coach. We call the trainer the "entrenador," but the Colombians use the English word.

Overall the team played the first half well, particularly the defense, who put the marking we'd practiced to good use. The forwards were a bit useless, but not all that bad. The first half was 0–0. In the second half we fell apart, and, despite my shouts and signals, our full-backs and center-half got blocked in. Two goals were scored against us.

If we want to be any good this afternoon, Pelao and I will have to play—he to lead the defense and me to push the ball forward so as to give the attackers more opportunities. We'll see.

It's now 10 p.m. and I'm soaking my feet in a bucket of warm water.

After this morning's game the day went like this: At midday we went to the Brazilian's. Arriving early, we mentioned how tempting it was to poke around in the forest not sticking to the path. Julinho, as he is called, showed us a tree with aerial roots clinging to the trunk, which, when struck with a branch, make a sound like a drum.

"Go and explore," he said, "and if you get lost call me like this, and I'll come and find you."

We accepted his suggestion. As we set out, I said to Pelao, "We're bound to get lost."

We walked for twenty minutes and took photos of some huge trees. When we started back by a path we thought was heading for the house, we realized it wasn't in fact the same one. So we decided to retrace our steps.

When we saw an anacahuita tree—that's the name of the tree with the strange roots—we got a stick and hit the trunk several times. Ten minutes went by (which seemed an age), and then Julinho appeared from a side-path, a big smile on his face.

Talking about how easy it is to get lost in the forest, we returned to the house. There were lots of young Brazilian girls and lads there. A pair of musicians on guitar and maracas played Brazilian sambas, Colombian porros and Peruvian waltzes.

We sat down to lunch. They serve it like the local Indians—that is, all the solid food is placed on plantain leaves on the ground. The soup and drinks are served in a vessel called a totuma, which is like a big maté gourd except that it comes from a tree, not—as in Argentina—from a creeper. Some totumas are the size of an orange, others more like a small pumpkin. The latter are used for serving soup.

There was lots of guinea-fowl stew, or perhaps it was of some similar bird with white feathers. It was delicious, and we ate tons. They offered us mazato, but since I hadn't forgotten how it's made, I wouldn't even look at it. So they broke open two coconuts and added a dash of cane brandy. It turned out to be a most agreeable drink. After our delicious lunch we bade farewell, since we had the soccer tournament to get back for.

It began at four, with knockout games of twenty minutes each way, with a five-minute rest. The finalists played two thirty-minute halves. We won our two matches, the first 2–0. I scored after five minutes, but I was still feeling full from lunch so I kept passing to my teammates. In the second game no one scored, thanks to Pelao in goal. Since we had three corners and only one against us, we won the round.

In the final both Pelao and I shone. The other side put two men on me, but they still couldn't get the ball away from me, and I always sent it to the best-placed player, but unfortunately three of these passes didn't turn into goals, as they should have.

The crowd applauded a lot. They nicknamed me "Little Pedernera," which I'm still feeling flattered by. But I think Fúser was the real hero of the afternoon, not just for his challenges, but also for the way he led the defense. Without him, two or three goals would have been scored against us.

As the game ended in a scoreless draw—and since it was the final—we went to penalties. Of their three kicks, one was a real cannonball and made it between the posts. The second went out, and the third Pelao saved brilliantly. It was well placed, heading straight for the upper right-hand corner of the net, but in an incredible stretch he tipped the ball over the crossbar.

Our penalties were taken by our center-forward, who sent them all wide. Despite our team coming second, we were the real heroes of the day, and everyone admired the change in Independiente Sporting after only a couple of days. People realized it wasn't just because of us, but because of the application of new, effective techniques. We've committed ourselves to a practice session tomorrow with anyone who wants it.

Leticia, 30 June 1952

This morning after some long, hard bargaining we sold the raft's lantern for three pesos to the regimental quartermaster. Then we went to wash our clothes in the river.

As promised yesterday, in the afternoon we had soccer

practice. At the end of the game, just as the flag was about to be lowered, Ernesto—who had been hit by the ball on the knee, where he had a previous injury—began looking for a piece of paper to stanch the blood. No sooner had the flag come down than the colonel burst into our midst and berated Fúser in the most offensive way for having moved during the ceremony. For a minute I feared that Fúser would respond as he ought to have, and I said to myself, "Goodbye, Colombia." But Ernesto swallowed his anger and kept his mouth shut. He always does the right thing.

Leticia, 1 July 1952

Today the plane arrived with a cable authorizing the two of us to travel on a single ticket. In the afternoon we were paid our coaching fees, which turned out to be forty Colombian pesos instead of thirty.

We sold the rest of the food that we had on the raft to the barracks quartermaster. As he knew we were leaving, he gave us fifteen pesos for what was worth more than fifty.

Bogotá—a city under siege

Bogotá, 2 July 1952

Iexperienced a new sensation today: my first airplane flight. Naturally, it had to be something out of the ordinary, and my debut as an air passenger was on a cargo seaplane, an amphibious twin-engine Catalina several decades old.

By 7 a.m. Ernesto and I were "perfectly positioned" in among the mailbags, soldiers' uniforms and bales of virgin rubber. Soon the engines started to roar. I was tense and expectant. How would my stomach react?

The plane began to skate over the river. There was a strong tail wind, so the plane had to do several runs until it finally got airborne; I watched the trees and the river sinking away below. We were flying, and a short while later we were at 10,000 feet.

We flew over forest for three hours. It looked for all the world like a cabbage field. The green was unbroken except for the occasional red crown of the bucare tree. The rivers were like labyrinths; their snaking bends splitting into a spider's web of tributaries. Breaking free of the clouds, the sun was a spectacular sight. The forest was partially flooded. The sun's reflection on this sea hidden within the foliage accompanied us like a spinning golden disc.

After three hours' flying we saw the plane fold its skis up to the wings and let down the landing gear. We were approaching Tres Esquinas. We got out. I had a sharp pain in my left knee, caused by the stress of the last few days on my meniscus lesion, so we stayed by the plane.

After refueling we continued on. After half an hour we reached the mountains. The cloud cover was thick, so the plane climbed to 14,000 feet. For a while we flew in cloud and to our delight the plane rattled and shook splendidly. As we reached an area of lower hills we left the cloud behind and the plane flew smoothly again. We flew over a small chain of bare low mountains and finally reached the savannah.

At first we followed the course of the Magdalena, with which we were familiar owing to our reading about South American rivers. Later we parted ways and flew straight across that immense uniformly green plain, marked only by the scars of roads.

At two that afternoon we reached Madrid, a military airfield about twenty miles outside Bogotá. We landed after some delicate maneuvers necessitated by the strong winds. From there we went on to Bogotá in a military truck. Leaving our gear in a Colombian Armed Forces warehouse, we set off for the Argentine embassy, where we were attended by the consul—for once a decent one. He treated us really well. He gave us letters from our families and found us lodgings on the university campus.

I am deliriously happy. We are in Bogotá. We have Colombian pesos earned in the most unlikely fashion (as soccer coaches). And, best of all, we have letters from home saying they are well and happy to hear of our adventures and to know that things have come off with relative ease. I am happy and feel sure there are no clouds on the horizon.

After saying goodbye to the consul we set off for the campus. It is located on the outskirts of the capital and surrounded by attractive parkland. The student halls of residence are housed in two buildings at the entrance.

Flanking the main avenue are the various faculties, each surrounded by trees and rose gardens. Finally one comes to the stadium and beside it the rector's office.

We were seen by the rector, who could offer us meals but not lodgings, as all the rooms are occupied by some UNESCO scholars. Later we went off to explore the city. Bogotá is situated more than 10,000 feet above sea level, flanked by bare hills that give the place a rather strange air.

The city center is colonial, with very narrow pavements and streets darkened by the tall buildings. Clearly the population has grown too large for the city and traffic is excessive. But the most surprising thing is the number of armed police all over the place. One can see that the government does not feel very secure. I don't like the atmosphere of this side of Colombia at all.

Bogotá, 3 July 1952

Yesterday afternoon, walking in the park behind the student residences, we came across a group of young people playing soccer. We asked to join in and played for a bit. But the altitude almost knocked me out. I could hardly run without gasping for breath. It's incredible how tired you can get from this thin air if you don't take time to adapt gradually.

The soccer players turned out to be a group of workers from a nearby factory. We chatted about soccer and told them some of the adventures we'd had along the way. They had a good laugh at some of our stories, but exchanged glances as if wondering whether or not to believe us.

At dusk we said farewell and went to have supper at the student canteen. For the first time in many weeks we sat at a table prepared in accordance with civilized custom. The supper was good. One thing however was strange.

They begin with either fresh fruit or a fruit cocktail, and then the savory dishes follow.

After supper I felt very tired. It dawned on me that in a matter of fourteen or fifteen hours we had gone from the tropical forest, at sea level, to the high plateau of the Andes; from the simple rustic life of the Amazon basin to a huge, complex metropolis. What a way to make the most of a day!

We left behind the light and warmth of the student dining hall to search for lodgings. It was drizzling lightly, which, after such a hectic day, made the night feel all the more pleasant for getting a good sleep. Soon, however, we were to find that something more was needed—a place to lay our heads.

First we went back to the army base where we had left our blankets. Everything was hermetically sealed. We went to several police stations—there was one on nearly every block—but were treated rudely and refused accommodation everywhere. After an unsuccessful attempt to bed down in a petrol station, we ended up at the San Juan de Dios hospital. It was already midnight. After convincing the night watchman to let us in, we found the doctor on duty. He was drunk as a skunk. At first he was suspicious and doubted we were colleagues, but then, with the affability of a drunk, offered us the best he had: two chairs. Apologizing for not being able to do better, he went away to sleep off his hangover.

We nodded off in the chairs until 6 a.m., then went out for breakfast. Later we went to meet Dr. Maldonado, to whom we had a letter of introduction from Dr. Pesce. Maldonado was fairly cordial. He introduced us to Dr. Serrano, head of the anti-leprosy campaign who, in turn, promised to give us a permit to lodge at the Santa Clara hospital. We were to come back at three that afternoon to collect it.

From there we went to the Millonarios soccer club to
say hello to some Argentine players. We found Banegas
and dropped a hint that we'd like tickets for the Sunday
match between Millonarios and Real Madrid. He pretend-
ed he hadn't understood.

We went back to the university for lunch. We remarked
to our table companions on the huge number of police on
campus. With much beating about the bush they told us
that there had been a student strike, which was savagely
put down by the government, and that the police had
behaved viciously.

After lunch we headed for the city center. Passing a
patch of grassy wasteland, we gave in to temptation and
lay down, for our hearty meal and lack of sleep the night
before had left us drowsy. We slept. Soon an unwelcome
drizzle obliged us to relinquish our "bedroom," and until
it let up we sheltered in a doorway. We found a little park
with several benches. I stretched out and slept while
Ernesto wrote his diary.

When I woke, we decided to go to the Argentine consulate. As we were quite disoriented we had the unfortunate idea of asking a policeman for directions. He then
started following us without our realizing it. After a few
blocks, as we couldn't agree on what route to take, Fúser
got out his gaucho knife, which is more a letter opener
than anything else, and began to trace a map on a wall.
The policeman, obviously attracted by the beauty of the
little silver dagger, came over and confiscated it.

After a short argument we decided to accompany him
to retrieve it. We had hardly gone a block when he decided to search us for weapons. Searching Fúser, the policeman found his allergy pills.

"Watch out," said Fúser, half sarcastic, half angry. "It's
a powerful poison!"

Why he had to say that I have no idea. We were taken

to a police station. The duty constable was very busy. He was playing dice with three other policemen. No matter how hard we tried, we couldn't get them to understand. In the end, in a bad temper, the constable said we were making fun of the Colombian police. Of course we denied it, and an argument ensued. He tried to end it by scaring us, but we told him to stop shouting and give us back the knife.

Luckily the sergeant arrived, and he was a shade less moronic than the others. He realized how ridiculous the whole thing was and told us to go and claim the knife at a central police station. He gave us the address.

Upon release we went to see Dr. Maldonado. He told us he could not get us accommodation in the Santa Clara hospital, but that he was going to try and get us lodging in the Instituto Lleras, an anti-leprosy clinic.

Today we spent the whole day trying to get a visa for Venezuela. The evening was spent discussing the leprosy law that allows infected individuals in the contagious stage of the disease to seek unregulated private treatment. I don't think Dr. Maldonado took kindly to our criticism.

Bogotá, 5 July 1952

Today we were victims of a shameful and terrible injustice. We went to the central police station, as we had been told to do, to retrieve the knife. While we were trying to explain our case to the duty sergeant, the constable who'd been so rude to us on Wednesday saw us and started to talk to a major who was lazing around doing nothing. The latter, after hearing him out, turned to us and in a loud, irritated voice told the sergeant dealing with us to draw up a warrant for our deportation for ridiculing the authorities.

It was pointless trying to say anything in our defense. The major turned on his heel, jumped into a car and shot off at high speed with his hand on the siren. Before we knew it, we were being thrown into an armored van. No one bothered to ask who we were or what we were doing. We crossed Bogotá in a novel mode of transport (one of the few we hadn't yet tried), and after being dragged through several offices where everyone washed their hands of us, we ended up in the local magistrate's court.

Once before the judge, rightfully indignant, we protested about the shameful way in which we—two foreigners with legal entry permits—had been treated. We asked him to phone Dr. Cuello, who duly told the judge who we were and exaggerated our merits. We were immediately released.

The incident caused us more mirth than anger. But the worst of it was really the overbearing attitude of the police. It appears that from the lowliest constable to the top officer they are accustomed to act in cases of this nature with impunity, exempt from having to answer to anyone for their outrages.

What upset us more than anything else was that when we commented on this issue of abuse of authority, whether on the university campus or with the Lleras hospital doctors, even if they condemned the police attitude they advised us to refrain from complaining as it could cause more problems. In other words, the government has achieved its objective—to tame and cow its citizens. But Fúser and I intend to fight on for the knife, not for the value of the thing, but to prove one should not choose the path of least resistance and condone intimidation.

Bogotá, 6 July 1952

All the museums and libraries are closed today, so we killed time watching a bicycle race. Forero, a Colombian, beat the favorite, Boyaert, a Frenchman.

We spent the afternoon at the Millonarios–Real Madrid match. It was a good game, in which the beauty of South

American play was set against the effective, although not exactly brilliant, strength and technique of European soccer. For Millonarios, Di Stefano was unbeatable, and Rossi, Pini, Báez and Cozzi all played well. I was surprised by the quality of Mourin, who never shone in Argentina as much as he did here today.

For the Spanish side the defense was outstanding, particularly the goalkeeper, Alonso, who effectively (if not gracefully) saved about five potential goals. I was also very impressed by Oliva, a midfielder who plays quite far back but handles the ball well. The other defender I liked was Muñoz, a veteran of the Spanish national team. As for the forwards, I liked the look of Molowny, from the Canary Islands, with his South American style, and Pahiño, a Galician with verve and courage, a real danger for the other side's forwards.

It was certainly a match well worth seeing. I can add it to my all-time favorites, which are not a lot, but not too few either.

We went to our lodgings early, having discovered once already that when the night watchman turns in it's impossible to wake him. He told us that the Mother Superior disapproved of our absence at Sunday mass.

Bogotá, 7 July 1952

This morning we went to Immigration to request an exit permit, and from there to the Argentine consulate about the knife. As the consul was not in, we decided to postpone it until tomorrow.

We went back to the university campus and talked to some students. They were well versed in politics and therefore open-minded. We discussed politics, literature and sport.

One of the good things I have encountered in this brief

stay in Colombia is Porfirio Barba Jacob's[1] poetry. Just as with Vallejo, in Peru, I'd never heard of him. No one knows these poets at home. Instead, we are made to study Menéndez y Pidal and dozens of European poets with whom we have nothing in common.

Bogotá, 8 July 1952

We spent the morning with Di Stefano. We talked about soccer, medicine and, finally, the sierras of Córdoba. He gave us some maté and two tickets for tomorrow's match.

The afternoon was taken up with arranging our visas for Venezuela. Then we returned to the Argentine consulate. At our request the consul called the police and once again we went to reclaim our knife. First we spoke to the judge and then the duty officer. The sergeant who had dealt with us on Saturday then joined in. He said he was going to call the constable involved and that we should return tomorrow afternoon for the knife.

In the evening we went to the university and sat talking with a group of architects who were there on UNESCO scholarships. A Uruguayan and two Venezuelans impressed us with their open, progressive ideas. They seem good lads. I only hope the Yankee octopus doesn't strangle them, as their UNESCO training means the organization will have priority in hiring them.

When we got back to our lodgings that night we found the room had not been made up. It seems the nuns are not very fond of us.

Bogotá, 9 July 1952

Today was a busy day. In the morning we went to the university, where we had been invited to play soccer. We left at eleven for the Campín stadium to see the second

---

[1] Porfirio Barba Jacob (1883–1942), Colombia's most influential poet, despite having spent most of his life in exile.

Millonarios–Real Madrid match. It was much like the first: grace and virtuosity on the part of the Latin Americans, while the Spaniards showed off their strength.

After the match we went to the police station. An officer dealt with us and, like all the others, tried to intimidate us, saying the matter was going to go to the Ministry of Defense, because we had ridiculed the authorities. He subjected us to the usual volley of insults.

Once again we vigorously refuted the charge. We made it clear that we would go wherever necessary to claim our rights. When faced with our insistence, we were shown into the commanding officer's office. He listened to us as though he was new to the whole affair, then dropped some hints about the danger of challenging the authorities, and then opened a drawer, and there was the knife. Fúser took it with undisguised pride. We diplomatically thanked the officer and left, happy with the outcome.

From there we went to the railway station to find out the price of a ticket to Agua de Dios. Then we went to the Ministry of Health to advise Dr. Maldonado of our intended trip. A huge surprise awaited us. Icily, he told us that he had sent a note to us at the Lleras Institute saying that the Ministry considered a trip to Agua de Dios to be beneficial neither to us nor to the state and was therefore not allowing us to visit the leprosarium.

We wanted an explanation, of course, but the doctor refused to discuss the matter further and ordered us to leave. After dinner we went to the Institute, where we were given the following note:

Messrs. Alberto Granado and Ernesto Guevara:

I am writing to inform you that this office has decided to refuse authorization for your visit to the Agua de Dios leprosarium. I would also request that you look elsewhere for your accommodation, since your stay at the Institute cannot be prolonged any further.

Sincerely yours,

Dr. Maldonado

In other words, a gratuitous, insulting way of kicking us out. We are both convinced that the change of attitude has to do with our criticism of the law on leprosy. There is no denying that the law has been drafted for the financial benefit of its champions. The unspeakable doctor's clinics are going full steam ahead, while the law allows people with leprosy bacillus to wander the streets and be treated in private sanatoria.

Bogotá, 10 July 1952

Once again this morning we had to go to the Venezuelan consulate. Then we went to bid farewell to the Argentine consul, thanking him for helping recover Fúser's knife.

Over lunch at the university, the architects and a group of students, who had taken up a collection, gave us 100 Colombian pesos. They also told us that two patrol cars had been round, with policemen asking about two Argentines without papers living in the university halls of residence. We were now being advised to leave, to take our things from the Institute and set out for Venezuela within hours. They also recommended that we not stay in any hotel or pension, since the policeman who tried to keep our knife and the officer who detained us, offended by the way things turned out, might try to make our lives difficult.

We left, remarking on the goodness of some people, who are ever ready to help those with their backs against the wall. We also talked about the fear that the present regime has instilled in the very bones of its citizens.

Later we went to the National Museum. It was interesting, for I'd been unaware of the influence of the Inca civilization in southern Colombia, whereas the civilization of the Indians in the east and north—for example, the tribes dwelling near the Venezuelan border in the Guajira—was and still is very primitive. There is also a beautiful collection of emeralds and gold artifacts from the Cocha civilization.

As it got dark we went to fetch our luggage. Fúser thought that our expulsion was nothing to do with politics, but because we hadn't accepted the Mother Superior's invitation to mass on Sunday. Just then we heard a police siren. We looked at each other and, as always, Pelao hit the nail on the head.

"Who knows how many sirens have wailed by in the last few days and we haven't even heard them," he said. "Now that we think they might be coming after us, they sound so gloomy."

"Shit, yeah, but just in case," I said, shouldering my knapsack, "let's take the advice we've been given and make ourselves scarce."

We headed for the coach station. The first departure for Cúcuta was at five in the morning. We left our gear in an office and prepared to spend the night wandering around.

We went to a cinema to see Curzio Malaparte's[2] *The Forbidden Christ*. On the surface it appears progressive, but one can see Malaparte's reactionary, fascist leanings.

After the film we went into a bar where we could hear a tango playing. We ordered beer. A rather colorful drunk soon came and sat with us. He said he was an admirer and friend of Pedernera and countless other Argentine soccer players. He kept repeating that Rossi was so popular that, if he were ever arrested, soldiers would shoot the prison director and civil war would be declared.

---

[2] *The Forbidden Christ*: Italian film written and directed in 1951 by controversial fascist author Curzio Malaparte (1898–1957).

We spent several hours listening to tangos and his drunken stories. The tangos came free, thanks to a trick of his. If you pressed the automatic button on the jukebox and at the same time banged it smartly against the wall, the record played as if you had put a coin in.

Málaga, 11 July 1952

Last night we chatted until four-thirty, then said goodbye to the Millonarios fan and went back to the coach station. The bus left on the dot of five and after a few blocks I was fast asleep. I woke around seven, when it began to get light. I felt happy and free. Ahead of us the road wound into the hills. The green fields, the blue sky, the cool breeze blowing through the coach made me feel euphoric.

Thankfully Bogotá was behind us now, with its police-infested streets, its hypocritical, grasping professionals, and its students, who though mainly generous and clear-thinking, were in the grip of fear. The Colombia we've seen is sorely in need of another reformer like Gaitán![3]

The countryside we passed through today is slightly like the Peruvian hills, but not as imposing. As we got closer to Málaga, the peaks grew higher, more arid and bare.

The passengers were mostly soldiers, and the conversation revolved around the rabble, or bandits, as they call the guerrillas fighting in the plains country.

It was painful to have to listen to them talking about the pleasure they got from seeing the planes, armed with large-caliber machine guns, blow the guerrilla fighters to bits, together with the rock they'd been using for cover. How can a people progress when, artificially divided into liberals and conservatives, they are sent to kill each other

---

[3] Jorge Eliécer Gaitán (1903–48), Colombian lawyer, sociologist and Liberal politician. He became President of Colombia in 1946 and was assassinated two years later.

off, all for the benefit of the oligarchy, who misrule and alternate power between the two parties?

Cúcuta, 12 July 1952

Last night we slept in Málaga, a rural town with nothing much to commend it. The usual town hall, church and park with benches engraved for small-town posterity with the name of a shopkeeper or apothecary who donated money for their construction.

On the coach we met a young Nicaraguan down on his luck, so we bought him dinner.

We slept in a boarding house for fifty Colombian centavos. Ernesto woke me around three in the morning with a terrible asthma attack. As luck would have it, we'd left the medicine in our luggage, so I had to wake the night watchman and then go back to the bus station. The watchman, like any self-respecting guard, was dead to the world, and it took some effort to rouse him.

I came back with the syringe and injected Ernesto with adrenalin. Then I slept again until six. Soon after, we continued our journey. We breakfasted in Pamplona. We reached Cúcuta at four in the afternoon only to find that we would not be seen until Monday as customs don't open on the weekend.

The Nicaraguan took us to a boarding house he knew. We installed ourselves and had dinner, but because of his asthma Ernesto barely ate. The Nicaraguan and I left him resting and went for a walk around town. When we got back Fúser was worse, so I gave him another adrenalin shot and said goodnight.

Cúcuta, 13 July 1952

Cúcuta is a typical cosmopolitan border town. At every step one bumps into people of every race doing every imaginable job. Always, of course, unhappy with where they come from or where they are, wishing to take off for greener pastures, which they'll also soon tire of, longing once more for new horizons.

It's quite hot here, but pleasant. This seems reflected in the local inhabitants who are cheerful and boisterous. Radios blare from every house, as do the shouts and laughter of their inhabitants. The streets are full of people hawking drinks, ice cream and sweets. They attract attention with songs, whistles or handclaps. In short, it's a typical tropical city, which has made me feel better about Colombia.

We spent the morning strolling around the outskirts, thick with mango trees and coconut palms, and the markets where you can buy anything from an air conditioner to a palm-fiber hammock. We saw some traders, called "ant smugglers," dress one of their small daughters, no older than ten, with six dresses, one on top of the other. The Nicaraguan, who's been here before, told us the girl probably has on ten bras and twenty pairs of knickers, which will be sold at much higher prices in Venezuela.

That afternoon we listened to the soccer match between the Brazilian team Botafogo and Millonarios, won by the former. We followed this with an evening of Colombian folk music, which was very nice, particularly the porros and all the tropical rhythms.

We had decided to tour the red-light district that night, but Fúser was still feeling bad with his asthma, so I had to inject him with adrenalin again. I'm a bit worried about this, because only a heart like Ernesto's is able to withstand the quantity I'm giving him.

However, once I saw him sleeping peacefully I couldn't resist and tiptoed out, woke the Nicaraguan, and we went off to the red-light district, which in fact is no more than a neighborhood of cheap boardinghouses where hundreds of wretched women wait for visas to enter Venezuela.

They all think they can get rich selling their bodies, and they dream about the money that will allow them to then leave behind this terrible profession.

There are beautiful women of all nationalities, even some Europeans, in particular Spanish, Italian and French; but the majority are Latin Americans: Cubans, Chileans, Argentines, Panamanians and of course lots of Colombians. They are all anxious to cross the border, which in their fantasies will bring them escape from their poverty or from the mediocrity of provincial life.

There are only two ways to get a visa: find money to pay a bribe or go to bed with someone influential. As I hadn't either cash or influence, I was left with the thankless task of remaining true to my principles, and in the least hurtful way possible I tried to show them the error of their ways. I told them stories about the white-slave trade in Argentina. I said they are victims of a social system that discriminates, exploits and uses them as merchandise.

The Nicaraguan, who dreams of becoming a millionaire by digging for diamonds in the upper Orinoco, felt threatened and tried to counter what I was saying with examples from the *Reader's Digest* about free trade, the newspaper boy who becomes a newspaper magnate, and so on. To my surprise most of the women agreed with me, although deep down they believe they can't fight their fate and must meekly resign themselves to it.

In the land of Bolívar

San Cristóbal, 14 July 1952

From now on this date will be not only a commemoration of the storming of the Bastille, but also of the day I left Colombia. Not the Colombia dreamed of by Bolívar or Gaitán, but that of Laureano Gómez,[1] which treated me a good deal less kindly than the sister countries I've come across so far.

Around seven in the morning we left for the Colombian–Venezuelan border. At nine we were attended to by an official who reactivated my anti-Colombian allergy. Finally, with a sigh of relief, we made it over the bridge that crosses the River Táchira and that joins the two countries. We were soon once more in the bureaucratic clutches of customs officers; this time they were Venezuelan.

After an hour of signing hundreds of papers, being fingerprinted and answering the same monotonous questions, we were through. Free at last, we reboarded the van that brought us here.

The road is quite pretty. We came over a small range of hills and after a two-hour journey reached San Cristóbal. It's like Cúcuta, but less cosmopolitan. The place is built on a series of hills. The streets are steep and generally peter out into small sugar-cane, cassava or banana plantations. The most picturesque scene is the River Torbes, its bright red waters contrasting with the green banks.

[1] Laureano Gómez (1889–1965), combative Colombian Conservative politician and reviled public figure, who was President from 1949 to 1951.

I'd like to stay a while in Venezuela. To start with, the Venezuelans have made a better impression on me than their neighbors. And an indicative detail—there is a good public library here in San Cristóbal, whereas in Cúcuta, a much larger place, a library is considered superfluous and unnecessary.

The road between Barquisimeto and Corona, 16 July 1952

We left San Cristóbal at eleven on Monday night. There were eleven of us in the van, packed in and very uncomfortable. I slept a lot.

The rising sun woke me at six. The highway was much like yesterday's, narrow and winding, bordered by banana plantations in the lowlands. Then the road climbed into immense arid wastelands, a monotony uninterrupted except by giant cactus. This region is called El Páramo.

We lunched in Puente Real for the astronomical price of two and half dollars each. The exchange rate makes living very expensive. In the afternoon we advanced up the incline very slowly owing to the excess weight the vehicle is carrying. To cap it all, we had three blowouts. The driver bought a new tire in Mérida, but, being lazy, had nothing done about the spare, so we had a fourth puncture. We lost almost two hours patching and mending the tires. The last straw was an icy wind, which is hardly typical of a tropical landscape.

We continued our ascent once the problem was solved and at around four came to Pico del Aguila, over 15,500 feet above sea level, where we had a meal. Then we immediately started the descent, and sleep descended too. I slept until seven in the morning. We were in the lowlands by then. The jungle encroached on the road, and it was quite hot. What a difference altitude makes in tropical regions!

We reached Barquisimeto by ten. This is quite a large

and seemingly prosperous town. We stopped briefly and had to watch the others quenching their thirst with beer while we drank water. The exchange rate is such that we have to think twice before buying anything. Of course, many of our temporary traveling companions offered to buy us drinks, but we had already accepted several invitations and it's uncomfortable to keep sponging.

Then on we went toward Valencia and around about eleven, bang! our fifth blowout. As we might have known, there's no spare. So the driver and some other lads got a lift and went off to the nearest town for a replacement. We decided to drink some maté and approached a house by the edge of the road. We found a black family, which startled us at first, since we'd come from the Andean region, where the Spanish and indigenous races predominate. Here we suddenly came face to face with what is a minority ethnic group in the South America we know.

While to the curiosity of all we sipped our maté, we remembered Rómulo Gallegos's[2] novel *Pobre Negro* and some of Bolívar's black lieutenants, and this mitigated our initial surprise. We moved on to discuss our plans for the immediate future. After analyzing the pros and cons, Ernesto and I have come to the conclusion that we have accomplished and gone beyond our initial idea of discovering Latin America. Of course, two major regions await us: Central America and Mexico. Both are politically and culturally important. The first, being an even clearer example of Yankee domination in what Aragón[3] termed "banana republics," one of which, Nicaragua, was Sandino's[4] birthplace.

[2] Rómulo Gallegos (1884–1969), Venezuelan writer, educator and politician, who was briefly President of the republic between February and November 1948.
[3] Agustín Aragón (1870–1954), Mexican engineer, positivist philosopher and essayist, who wrote about the evolution of popular language in his country.
[4] Augusto "César" Sandino (1895–1934), charismatic Nicaraguan nationalist and anti-imperialist guerrilla leader. He was betrayed by the President, after signing a ceasefire, and assassinated by the National Guard.

Mexico, cradle of the first agrarian revolution, also deserves a visit. Besides, Central America, with its Mayan civilizations, and Mexico, with the Aztecs, can teach us a thousand interesting things. On the other hand, we are not professional globetrotters, and at some point we have to sit down and do something useful. Therefore we decided the following:

If a certain dealer in racehorses here in Caracas—an associate of one of Pelao's uncles—will take him on the plane in which he transports his horses, then Pelao will return to Buenos Aires to finish his medical degree. I will stay here in Venezuela working either in a leprosarium or at the university with one of the professors to whom I have letters of introduction. Otherwise we will continue on to Mexico.

Three or four hours went by as we drank maté and discussed these questions. Finally the driver and his assistant returned with the repaired tires.

Caracas, 17 July 1952

Caracas is an attractive modern city. Both Pelao and I were fed up with the setbacks on the road. But when we arrived at a village called Los Teques, the road began to climb, flanked by wooded hills. We saw pine forests or perhaps monkey-puzzle trees, which one is more likely to come across in the Andes than in these low tropical hills. Then we entered a narrow valley at the end of which we glimpsed tall buildings.

The traffic increased as soon as we got near the city. We began to see long lines of cars of many makes and sizes fighting to overtake each other and creating an unbelievable chaos. Such a contrast to the peace and beauty of the road only a few miles back!

We stayed in Caño Amarillo, having been told it was the place for cheap lodgings. Fúser had another asthma attack coming on, so we found a room as quickly as possible. But all we could afford was a dump, where I left Ernesto resting while I, after ironing my battered suit, went in search of the Argentine embassy.

After much difficulty I finally managed to speak to some embassy officials. Real icebergs they were, disguised as human beings and pathologically afraid I was going to ask for money for food. I collected the letters in my name, but they wouldn't give me Pelao's. After listening to them go on and on about how hard life is in Venezuela and how we'd be better off moving on as fast as possible before we ran out of money—what little we might have had, judging from the way I looked—I left almost without saying goodbye, since I was about to tell them all to go to hell.

I went back to the boardinghouse with a long face, but arrived to find Fúser somewhat recovered.

That afternoon we went to look for a friend's aunt, a Miss Margarita Calvento. She turned out to be a real gem, and when I told her what had happened at the embassy she suggested—and we agreed—that because of my appearance they hadn't believed a word I said. A few hours later, we had confirmation of this. After a sumptuous mid-afternoon feast, Margarita proposed that we visit a student boardinghouse, the Venezuelan Young Catholics, no less.

Armed with a letter of introduction and after checking out each other's presentableness, we arrived at the aforesaid place. Obviously we didn't look all that great, because the manageress, under our very eyes, rang Margarita Calvento to ask whether she had sent a letter of introduction with a Dr. Granado and a Mr. Guevara. Of course, I didn't hear what our compatriot replied, but I suspect she had to wax lyrical to convince that old bird that, despite our appearance, we were indeed what she said we were in her letter.

Caracas, 18 July 1952

Today we went to the home of the representative of the racehorse dealer. Ernesto's uncle is his customs agent in Buenos Aires. He is happy for Ernesto to do the Caracas–Miami–Buenos Aires journey as long as he can get a US transit visa.

Margarita, a sort of spinsterish fairy godmother, is going to put us into contact with an Argentine journalist who represents the United Press International (UPI) in Caracas and therefore has good relations with the Yankee embassy.

Caracas, 19 July 1952

We went to meet Dr. Convit, to whom we had a letter of introduction from Dr. Pesce, to see if he could get me work. He received us warmly and, although he was a man of few words, within five minutes he gave me the once-over, albeit disguised as questions on my medical experience. I liked him, and when he offered me 500 bolívares plus accommodation in the hospital, I had to control myself not to say yes on the spot. However, keeping to my plan, I said I'd think about it, forcing myself to appear indifferent in spite of Fúser's desperate signals for me to accept.

A family gathering

Today, while Fúser went to the Yankee embassy along with Leguizamón, the journalist, I went to the university, which is one of the other places where they might give me work.

The campus is very attractive. Surrounded by high fences, it contrasts with the poverty of the huts that crown the little neighboring hills. The teacher to whom I had been recommended, a physiologist, was out of the country in Canada. I spoke to several students and, in spite of an undercurrent of apprehension, was told that he and other valuable teachers have had to leave the university because of their progressive ideas.

There were a lot of police about and an unpleasant atmosphere in general. But nonetheless I very much liked the open, easy Venezuelan style. They use the familiar "tú" as soon as they meet you, and so far I've seen nothing of the xenophobia people warned us about.

In the afternoon I went to see Dr. Convit and asked him where the job would be. He told me it was in the hospital at Cabo Blanco, about twenty miles from Caracas, and that he would come and pick me up the next day in a van to take me to see it.

That night we gathered at Miss Calvento's, where we met two Argentine women who work and live with her. We spent a long while recounting some of our adventures and chatting with Ernesto about how easy it had turned out to be for him to get a visa, thanks to Leguizamón's help. As we were speaking, Leguizamón arrived with his wife. We drank a toast to our arrival and to Fúser's imminent departure.

Our farewell was not all peace and good omens, however. The UPI man was determined to needle us by talking about the marvels of the United States and the inferiority of the Latin peoples. For a while, because he had helped us, Fúser and I put up with the nonsense he was talking, until he said it was a pity the Argentines had defeated the English in 1806, otherwise we'd be like the Americans.

"Or like the Indians," I leaped in to say, "with a ninety percent malnutrition and illiteracy rate, after five hundred years of English colonialism."

Pelao turned to me and said, "Well, I'd rather be an illiterate Indian than a North American millionaire."

Everyone present who had come to Venezuela with the secret hope of becoming at least rich took it personally, but of course the "brilliant" journalist took it upon himself to have the leading say. He began with the most pathetic stories of poor people who by their own efforts have made themselves millionaires.

First we laughed in his face, and then we began to tell him about what we had just experienced during our journey. About the wages, about currency devaluation, about overseas loans that go to those countries that the cartels decide to help. After ten minutes I sat down to enjoy my glass of wine. With his arguments, his sarcasm and his depth of analysis, Pelao was more than a match for all of them, and I was more of a hindrance than a help.

In a slightly calmer mood we said goodbye and left for our respectable guesthouse. On the way I said, "If he could, that guy would cancel your visa."

Caracas, 21 July 1952

Today we went to the leprosarium. The road between Caracas and La Guaira is strikingly beautiful. It seems this whole landscape was once full of coffee plantations, with different trees for shading the coffee, which makes for a great variety of foliage. This winding road—which offers great views over the matchless blue of the Caribbean—snakes its way between high precipices, not quite the Peruvian Andes, but still dangerous, being so narrow and full of curves.

The driver told me the road had been built by political prisoners in the time of the dictator Juan Vicente Gómez[1] and followed the route of an old mule track. It's a nice joke, and the number of unnecessary curves lends it credibility.

The hospital is a veritable witches' den—ugly, dilapidated and unpainted—but situated only a few steps from the sea. A beach of pure-white sand comes right up to the fence, with surf that would delight any vacationer.

Caracas, 22 July 1952

Yesterday's visit to the hospital gave us a glimpse into a future full of valuable research work. The director-general, Dr. Convit, and Dr. Blumenfeld, who is head of the laboratory, both seem prepared to listen and to give me a free hand in everything related to research, so it seems that prospects look promising.

25 July 1952

Fúser leaves early tomorrow, bound for his future. He has to study hard to finish his degree.

After so many months together, it is hard to part. We are both trying not to show the sadness that overwhelms

---

[1] Juan Vicente Gómez (1857–1935), Venezuelan dictator who dominated political life in his country from 1908 until his death.

us. But after all, our separation is only temporary. I know we'll be together again soon.

Just as ten years ago I had the certainty that we would make this journey, so I have the same certainty now that Fúser and I will travel the same path together in the future.

Epilogue

Once in Venezuela we decided to travel on to Caracas, where I met a doctor who had read some of my research on Hansen's disease and who offered me work in the clinical laboratory of a leprosy hospital.

This event, coupled with the fact that a friend of Ernesto's family was in Caracas and had a plane for transporting racehorses, gave rise to the pact between Che and I that he would return to Buenos Aires, thus fulfilling the promise I had made to his mother, Celia de la Serna, that Ernesto would go back and graduate.

I had to insist that Ernesto went back to Buenos Aires. He left for Miami, where he had to stay for a while enduring some hardships. We parted in July 1952 and were only able to shake hands again on 18 July 1960, when I visited him at the Banco Nacional de Cuba.

The plane's itinerary was: Buenos Aires–Caracas, Caracas–Miami, Miami–Maracaibo–Buenos Aires. It carried Argentine horses to be sold in Miami; there it picked up American horses and sold them in Maracaibo. Che had to take advantage of that plane ride, in spite of the many stopovers, because it was an inexpensive way of traveling.

Che told us that in Miami he had had a tough time; he would go to the public library frequently, and his only meal was a daily milky coffee, until he made friends with the owner of a diner and the latter would offer him something to eat—until one lunchtime a Puerto Rican arrived and started to slag off the Truman government, and an FBI agent overheard him and the usual happened: Che had to keep his distance.

I was concerned that he should graduate. And with his peculiar study methods and his rare capacity and intelligence, he was able to pass eleven or twelve exams in less than a year. Che graduated in medicine in March 1953.

Once he had graduated, he embarked on a trip to meet up with me in Venezuela to decide if we should continue with our journey or take up some sort of research at Cabo Blanco, the leprosarium where I was employed. He didn't want to borrow money from anybody and managed on what he had; he thought it was more romantic to do things his own way.

With two or three friends, he boarded a train that travels from Buenos Aires to La Paz in Bolivia, a journey of some 4,000 miles. A train that stops at every single city, great or small. A terrible journey.

He then crossed Lake Titicaca, where we had been when we traveled together, and carried on along the coast because he wanted to reach Venezuela quickly.

However, when he reached Guayaquil in Ecuador, he met Ricardo Rojo, a lawyer from Buenos Aires, who was in exile, having escaped from jail in a spectacular breakout. He had asked for asylum at the Guatemalan embassy in Buenos Aires and a diplomat had escorted him to Guatemala.

Rojo, who had not met Guevara before, said something that made Che change his mind.

When Ernesto told Rojo of his intention to continue on to Caracas, to meet up with me and take up a job of some sort, Rojo said, "But, Guevara, how can you go to Venezuela, a worthwhile country only if it's dollars you're after? Come with me to Guatemala, where a real social revolution is taking place."

In view of that plan, I got a note from Ernesto that read: "Petiso, I'm off to Guatemala. I'll write to you."

I learned about the triumph of the Cuban revolution during a visit to the Guevara household. It was 31 December and Jorge Ricardo Masetti, who was among the dinner guests invited by Doña Celia, Ernesto's mother, brought the news.

In reply to a letter from me, Che wrote the following:

Military Department of La Cabaña,
La Habana, 11th March 1959

Mial,

Although I was expecting it, your letter gave me great pleasure. I did not write to you until now from this my new country because I had planned to go to Venezuela with Fidel. Other events prevented me from doing so. I meant to go a little later, but I am ill and bed-ridden. I hope to go in approximately one month's time.

You were in my thoughts to such an extent that when I was invited to Venezuela I demanded two free days to spend with you and yours. I hope this wish becomes a reality soon.

I won't reply to the cheap philosophy of your letter because that would require a couple of matés, a little empanada[1] and a shady corner under a tree. Then we will talk.

I send you the biggest hug that your macho dignity allows you to receive from another one.

Che

Before leaving Cuba for the last time, Che sent me a book with this dedication:

---

[1] Empanada: a traditional Argentine meat pasty.

Havana, year of agriculture

Alberto,
I don't know what to leave you as a memento.
So I'll oblige you to devote yourself to the sugar
economy.[2] My itinerant home will be off on two
legs once again and my dreams shall know no
bounds, at least until bullets decide otherwise . . .
I'll be expecting you, sedentary gypsy, when the
smell of gunpowder subsides. A hug for all of you
(Tomás included).
Che

[2] The dedication was written by Guevara in the first page of a book about the
Cuban sugar-cane industry and sent to the author in March 1965 on the eve of
Che's departure for Congo.

Chronology

1922

8 August: Hernando, province of Córdoba, Argentina—Alberto Granado Jiménez is born to Dionisio T. Granado, a Spanish clerical employee of the Argentine railway system, and Adelina Jiménez Romero. Alberto is the first of three sons.

1928

14 June: Rosario, province of Santa Fé, Argentina—Ernesto Guevara de la Serna is born to Ernesto Guevara Lynch and Celia de la Serna, both of distinguished "founding families," politically radical and active. He is the first of five children.

1930

Ernesto suffers the onset of asthma, a lifelong condition.

6 September: General Uriburu topples the popular and nationalist government of Hipólito Irigoyen, and Alberto's father, who has been a militant trade unionist, is advised to leave the area. The family moves to Villa Constitución in the province of Santa Fé.

1931

Alberto's mother suffers from ill heath and he is sent to live with his paternal grandparents in Córdoba where he continues his studies.

1934
For the sake of Ernesto's health, the Guevara family moves to Alta Gracia in the province of Córdoba, famous for its mountain air.

1936
Alberto begins studying for the baccalaureate at the Colegio Nacional Dean Funes.

1940
Alberto attends the University of Córdoba where he studies chemistry and biochemistry.

1941–42
The Guevara family moves to the city of Córdoba, capital of the province. Ernesto begins studying for the baccalaureate at the Colegio Nacional Dean Funes. Ernesto and Alberto meet. Despite bouts of illness Ernesto is a diligent student and a keen sportsman. He also takes advantage of the family's huge library, and reads widely in literature, philosophy and politics. He is much involved in the family's political activities.

1943
Granado is jailed for taking part in a political movement against the dictatorship of General Juan Perón. He is released the following year.

1945–51
The Guevara family moves to Buenos Aires. Ernesto enrolls in the School of Medicine at the University of Buenos Aires. Aside from his studies, he works as a volunteer in an allergy research institute. He goes on long bicycle trips during the winter holidays (June–September) round the northwest of Argentina, a total of over 2,900

miles. The bicycle was important to him, for educating the will and discovering the landscape on a human scale. In 1950 he serves as a deckhand on a steamer and travels through Panama, Honduras and Haiti.

1946
Granado earns an MSc in chemistry at the University of Córdoba. He wins the position of medical assistant to the Chair of the Hygiene and Epidemiology Department.

1947–51
Granado is Director of Pharmacology and Clinical Laboratory at the San Francisco del Chañar leprosarium. He earns an MSc in biochemistry at the University of Córdoba and obtains a scholarship to the Instituto Malbrán in Buenos Aires, famous for its laboratories and library.

1951
29 December: Guevara and Granado set out by motorbike to visit some of the Pacific-coast countries. Both keep diaries.

1952
January–June: In Peru they stay at the leper colony of San Pablo, then travel on the Amazon to Colombia. In Bogotá the two are detained and interrogated by the forces of dictator Laureano Gómez; they leave to avoid further trouble. July: They reach Caracas, Venezuela. Guevara hitches a ride to Buenos Aires via Miami on board a transport plane. In Miami, he gets stuck for a month due to lack of funds and experiences the United States of America for the first time. Granado remains in Venezuela and works at the laboratory of the Cabo Blanco leprosarium in Maiquetía.

10 March 1952: Military strongman Fulgencio Batista succeeds in a right-wing coup d'état in Cuba.

1953

March: Guevara graduates in medicine. His thesis on allergies is prompted by his asthma. He is called up for national service, but declared unfit for active duty.

26 July: Fidel Castro leads insurgents against Batista. Their attack on the Moncada garrison in Santiago de Cuba fails and there are heavy casualties; Castro and other survivors are later captured and imprisoned.

July: Start of Guevara's second trip across Latin America. With Calica Ferrer, Guevara takes the train from Buenos Aires to La Paz, a journey of 4,000 miles.

December: Guevara arrives in Guatemala, where President Jacobo Arbenz leads the country's elected left-wing government.

1954

January–June: Unable to find a medical post Guevara takes odd jobs, studies Marxism and is politically active. He meets exiled Cuban revolutionaries.

June: Mercenary forces backed by the CIA invade Guatemala City; Guevara volunteers to fight; President Arbenz refuses to arm the population and resigns.

September: Guevara flees from Guatemala and arrives in Mexico City, where he works as a doctor at the Central Hospital. He writes his first political article: "I Saw the Fall of Jacob Arbenz."

1955

July: Having been released from detention in Cuba in response to public pressure, Fidel Castro arrives in Mexico.

July–August: Guevara meets Castro, is confirmed as the third member of the future guerrilla expedition, and starts training recruits. Guevara becomes known as "Che."

18 August: Guevara marries Peruvian economist Hilda Gadea.

Granado obtains a scholarship to the Istituto Superiore di Sanità in Rome, Italy. During his stay in Europe he visits Spain, France and Switzerland. Upon his return he marries Delia María Duque Duque.

1956

24 June: Guevara and Castro are arrested by the Mexican authorities together with twenty-eight Cuban recruits.

25 November: Having been released from jail, Castro, Guevara and eighty men leave Mexico on the yacht *Granma* for Cuba.

2 December: They land at Belic and are surprised by Batista's troops at Alegría de Pío. Only seventeen men from the landing regroup.

1957

17 January: Attack on La Plata. First Rebel Army victory. Although officially the doctor for the rebel forces, Guevara takes part in the fighting.

Between January and May the rebel army wins battles at Arroyo del Infierno, Palma Mocha and El Uvero.

5 June: Guevara is made Commandant of the Fourth Column to disguise the fact that there are only two, the first under the command of Fidel Castro himself.

1958

July: The rebels win the battle of El Jigüe, a decisive victory.

December: The rebel forces now control half of Cuba.

Guevara and his men win the battle of Santa Clara on 31 December.

When the Venezuelan dictator Pérez Jiménez is ousted, Granado is put in charge of the reorganization of the School of Bio-analysis at the University of Caracas, where he works until 1961.

31 December: Granado is visiting Argentina with his family. While dining in Buenos Aires with Guevara's mother, they hear of the triumph of the Cuban Revolution.

1959

1 January: President Batista flees Cuba.

2 January: Guevara's column enters Havana and occupies La Cabaña fortress.

8 January: Fidel Castro arrives in Havana after a week's victory tour of the island.

9 February: Guevara is declared a Cuban citizen in recognition of his contribution to Cuba's liberation.

16 February: Castro becomes Prime Minister. He and Guevara embark on an extensive program of economic and social reforms.

2 June: Guevara and Hilda Gadea divorce amicably and Guevara marries Aleida March who has been his aide for some months.

June–September: As a representative of the government, Guevara goes on a long tour through Europe, Africa and Asia.

7 October: Guevara is put in charge of Agrarian Reform.

26 November: Guevara is appointed Governor of the Cuban National Bank, with total responsibility for the country's finances. He then starts studying higher mathematics.

1960

17 March: Under orders from President Eisenhower, the CIA commences training Cuban exile volunteers for an invasion of Cuba.

8 May: The USSR recognizes Cuba's revolutionary government.

June–December: Cuba nationalizes the oil refineries. In response Eisenhower reduces US trade in sugar. The USSR takes up the surplus. Relations between the US and Cuba deteriorate. Nationalization of major US companies, foreign-owned banks and privately owned Cuban companies. Guevara visits the German Democratic Republic, Czechoslovakia, the USSR, China and the People's Democratic Republic of Korea.

Invited by Guevara, Granado travels to Cuba for the first time.

1961

January–February: Total breakdown in relations between US and Cuba.

23 February: Guevara is appointed Minister for Industry.

March: Granado moves to Cuba with his family and works as professor of medical biochemistry in the School of Medicine of the University of Havana.

15 April: US planes attack Santiago de Cuba and Havana.

16 April: Castro announces the revolution's commitment to socialism.

17 April: 1,500 counter-revolutionaries, with full US official support, invade Cuba at Playa Girón (Bay of Pigs); Guevara commands troops at Pinar del Río province.

19 April: Last counter-revolutionaries surrender at Playa Girón.

8 August: Guevara speaks at the Organization of American States' (OAS) Inter-American Economic and Social Conference in Punta del Este, Uruguay, and denounces the American Alliance for Progress. Family and friends cross over from Buenos Aires to meet up with him. He slips across the frontier for a secret meeting in Buenos Aires with President Arturo Frondizi, which results in Frondizi being ousted by the military.

December: Cuba completes a year-long nationwide literacy campaign. Guevara's book *Guerrilla Warfare—a Method* is published in Cuba.

Granado is one of the founders of the Institute for Basic and Pre-Clinical Sciences.

1962

January: The Organization of American States votes to expel Cuba.

February: President Kennedy orders total embargo on US trade with Cuba. Cuba issues Second Declaration of Havana underlining Cuba's support for revolutionary struggle throughout the Americas.

27 August–7 September: Guevara makes a second visit to the Soviet Union as the head of an economic delegation.

October: Cuban Missile Crisis—Guevara occupies his combat position in command of Pinar del Río province. Nikita Khrushchev agrees to remove Soviet missiles from Cuba in exchange for US pledge not to invade the country. Granado and a group of colleagues found Cuba's second Faculty of Medicine at the University of Santiago.

1963

January: Guevara's mother arrives in Havana to visit her son, with whom she tours the island.

July: Guevara sets out for Algeria to represent the Revolutionary Government at the ceremonies commemorating the first anniversary of Algerian independence.

December: Guevara delivers closing speech of the Week of Solidarity with South Vietnam.

1964

March: Guevara leaves for Geneva, Switzerland, as head of the Cuban delegation to the UN Conference on Trade and Development, and later addresses the Conference in plenary session.

4–19 November: Guevara attends celebrations marking 47th anniversary of October Revolution in the USSR. He meets the Vietnamese leader Ho Chi Minh.

11 December: As President of the Cuban delegation Guevara addresses the XIX United Nations General Assembly in New York.

17 December: Guevara leaves New York for Africa, where he spends three months. He visits Algeria, Mali, Dahomey, Congo-Brazzaville, Ghana, Tanzania and Egypt before returning to Cuba in March 1965.

1965

1 April: Guevara leaves Cuba to head an internationalist mission in Congo, leaving his letter of resignation with Fidel Castro.

December: Guevara returns to Cuba in secret.

1966

July: Pinar del Río province—Guevara selects the Cuban Internationalist detachment for a mission to Bolivia.

7 November: Guevara arrives at the site of his Bolivian camp with seventeen Cubans, and several Bolivian recruits.

1967

23 March: First successful guerrilla military action against Bolivian army column.

16 April: Guevara's Message to the Tricontinental Conference of Solidarity for the Peoples of Africa, Asia and Latin America, taking place in Havana, calls for "two, three, many Vietnams."

May–October: A massive force of Bolivian troops and US advisers closes in on Guevara's guerrillas, who suffer heavy losses.

8 October: Guevara is wounded and captured by government troops.

9 October: Guevara is executed in the village of La Higuera.

15 October: Castro confirms that Guevara is dead and declares three days of official mourning in Cuba.

16 December: Granado is transferred to Havana, where he is one of the founders of the National Health Center for Stockbreeding and Farming, becoming director of the Department of Genetics.

1970–74

Granado carries out scientific research, lectures in Cuba and abroad and is appointed senior professor.

1975–86

Granado obtains a doctorate in biological sciences. He is centrally involved in developing the Holstein Tropical cattle breeds. He attends the World Congress on Genetics in Moscow and the Congress on Polymorphism in Leningrad.

1986–90
Granado takes part in the creation and organization of the Cuban Genetics Society, and is appointed its president.

1991–94
Granado devotes himself to the validation and methodology of his research in leading universities in Spain and Venezuela. He retires in 1994.

1997
The remains of Guevara and some of his comrades in arms are dug up at the airstrip of Vallegrande in Bolivia and returned to Cuba.
12 July: Guevara and his comrades are buried with full military honors in the city of Santa Clara, in the province of Las Villas, where Guevara won the decisive battle of the Cuban Revolution. Granado joins the campaign for solidarity with Cuba and the promotion of Guevara's ideas in Cuba and abroad.

2002–3
Granado acts as adviser to Walter Salles, director of the film *The Motorcycle Diaries*, which is based on Guevara's and his own account of their journey, on location in Argentina, Chile and Peru.